ONE PAN
& DONE

ALSO BY MOLLY GILBERT

Sheet Pan Suppers

ONE PAN & DONE

HASSLE-FREE MEALS FROM THE OVEN TO YOUR TABLE

MOLLY GILBERT

CLARKSON POTTER/PUBLISHERS

NEW YORK

TO AUNT BABE,
the original "MG," for
always being there, both in
the kitchen and out.

AND TO BEN AND CALDER,
for making life
delicious.

Copyright © 2017 by Molly Gilbert
Photographs copyright © 2017 by Aran Goyoaga

All rights reserved.
Published in the United States by Clarkson Potter/Publishers,
an imprint of the Crown Publishing Group, a division of
Penguin Random House LLC, New York.
crownpublishing.com
clarksonpotter.com

CLARKSON POTTER is a trademark and POTTER with colophon
is a registered trademark of Penguin Random House LLC.

Library of Congress Cataloging-in-Publication Data
Names: Gilbert, Molly, author.
Title: One pan and done / Molly Gilbert.
Description: First edition. | New York: Clarkson Potter, 2017 |
Includes index.
Identifiers: LCCN 2016015775| ISBN 9781101906453 (trade pbk.) |
ISBN 9781101906460 (ebook)
Subjects: LCSH: Roasting (Cooking) | Broiling. | Baking. | One-dish
meals. | LCGFT: Cookbooks.
Classification: LCC TX690 .G55 2017 | DDC 641.7/1—dc23
LC record available at https://lccn.loc.gov/2016015775.

ISBN 978-1-101-90645-3
Ebook ISBN 978-1-101-90646-0

Printed in China

Design by Laura Palese

10 9 8 7 6 5 4 3 2

First Edition

CONTENTS

INTRODUCTION

They call me the Sheet Pan Queen.

I mean, okay, I don't have a shiny crown or anything, and truth be told, I've only been called that once in my life (and it was by a family member, so I'm not even sure it counts), but for a few years now, cooking meals on a sheet pan has kind of been my thing. My first cookbook, *Sheet Pan Suppers,* focused on simple, flavorful meals pulled straight from the oven on a sheet pan. No mess, no fuss, plus the easiest cleanup on the block. Sounds pretty nice, right? (It is.) But can I tell you a secret?

I have more than one kind of pan in my kitchen. Oh, and also? Sometimes I want to eat soup.

. . . STOP THE PRESSES AND CALL OPRAH, PLEASE.

But really, why should sheet pans have all the fun? Doesn't your mom's old Dutch oven deserve some glory? Doesn't that trusty glass baking dish work hard for the money? The answers are: They definitely shouldn't. It does. And yes, it really does. So this go-round, we're focusing on simple, flavorful meals pulled straight from your oven . . . on a sheet pan, in a Dutch oven, a cast iron skillet, a glass or ceramic baking dish, even cake pans and muffin tins! We've got a whole arsenal of cooking vessels to work with—and after years of straight sheet pans, I feel like a sophomore on spring break in Cancún . . . with a muffin tin. Or something. The point is, in *One Pan & Done* you'll find a cache of simple, smart, and flavorful dishes that use just ONE pot or pan, in a totally fuss-free and (mostly) hands-off method. Because who has time for fussy? Not me.

In truth, I cook this way because it's how I like to eat—simply, elegantly, heavy on comfort but also on health, without too much cleanup. And I find that most people, whether overscheduled parents, busy young professionals, or even the accomplished cooks I know who are well versed in the art of the dinner party, agree. Because, at its heart, food is about comfort, nourishment, family, and community. It's about bringing people to the table and *enjoying* a shared experience. And even when I'm eating alone, I think it's important to take time to savor and enjoy. So making an elaborate meal, pulling out ALL of my kitchen equipment, trying to tame four pots at once, and still keep the kitchen clean, all while simultaneously charming my dinner guests or chasing after my son or just debriefing the day's events with my husband, just doesn't work. In my mind, a handful of great ingredients treated simply and respectfully, one pot or pan, and the occasional helpful shortcut (like store-bought biscuit dough) are where is at.

In *One Pan & Done* I will show you how to use your oven to your advantage, letting it do most of the work to turn out juicy, crispy roasts, succulent vegetables, rich stews, flaky fish, and, of course, the occasional (likely chocolaty, maybe fruity, possibly crumbly, probably buttery) sweet treat. Covering everything from brunch, starters, and snacks and sides to vegetarian main dishes, meat, fish, poultry, and sweets, my goal here is to give you the best of both worlds—the deeply roasted goodness of sheet pan suppers plus the rich comfort of soups, stews, and pasta, too. And the loveliest part is that with our simple, hands-off approach, you'll be able to take time to hang out with your family (or catch up on *Game of Thrones*) during weeknight dinner prep, and actually enjoy the company of your guests at the party you're throwing.

Sheet Pan Queen? I'll take it. But I'd rather be *One Pan & Done*.

THE ONE PAN 411

• HOW IT WORKS •

So how exactly can you use this book? Great question. I've done my best to pull together a collection of recipes, from brunch to appetizers and side dishes, from hearty meals to desserts, that cook in your oven in ONE single pot or pan. The objective here is ease, simplicity, minimal dish pileup, and as much hands-off cooking time as possible. It's this laid-back oven method (throwing one pan in the oven so that dinner—or brunch, dessert, what have you—can cook itself) that makes *One Pan & Done* stand out from the crowd, and it's a method that, come mealtime, I feel confident you'll appreciate.

Many recipes in this book call for simply assembling your dish in a pan and then sliding it into the oven to cook (see the Simple Chicken Cassoulet, page 145; Roasted Shrimp and Chickpea Salad, page 152; or Broiled Beef and Broccoli, page 201, for example)—these are the ultimate in hands-off cooking, which, as far as we're concerned, is the name of the game.

Others will start on the stovetop and finish in the oven, which lets us do things like get a nice, crusty sear on our Pan-Roasted Pork Chops with Butternut Squash, Tomatoes, and Sage (page 194) or perfectly crisp skin on the Halibut with Wilted Greens and Citrus Salsa (page 155), and sweat onions until brown and fragrant as for the Linguine Primavera (page 109). These dishes all finish in the oven, though, because taking advantage of the even, circulating heat in there is helpful both for our food and our sanity. Instead of compulsively standing over a Dutch oven, trying (and, in all likelihood, failing) to resist the urge to uncover and stir the pot every five minutes, with this stovetop-to-oven method we can simply close the oven door and walk away until our perfectly cooked meal is done. It's the "out of sight, out of mind" version of getting dinner on the table, posthaste.

A small handful of recipes here, mainly the soups, cook entirely on the stovetop, but something about soup just screams low fuss, don't you think? The ones I've included here are some of my favorite quick and simple meals. They come together without much bother or fanfare (read: hands-on cook time), but are heavy on flavor and comfort. *One Pan & Done* indeed!

• A WORD ON YOUR OVEN •

A quick word of warning: Don't trust your oven. Whether it's old and run-down or brand-spanking-new, odds are your oven is yanking your chain in one way or another. Maybe it takes forever to preheat, or says it's running at 400°F when it's actually only 325°F in there, or maybe the front runs hotter than the back. Depending on the make, model, vintage, and general eccentricity of your particular appliance, these are common issues, although happily, they're easily fixable. I recommend buying a cheap oven thermometer (a little stainless steel number that either sits or hangs inside your oven) to help you get to know what you're working with, ovenwise. Once you've gotten to know the quirks of your particular appliance, you can compensate appropriately (by setting your oven to 450°F instead of 400°F when you know it runs cool by 50°F, for example, or by rotating your tray of cookies to ensure an even bake).

• A PRIMER ON POTS & PANS •

So how exactly can we be *One Pan & Done*? With a small arsenal of trusty pots and pans in our corner, that's how. Marked with a handy symbol, each recipe throughout the book will indicate what pan you'll be using. Let's meet our heavy hitters.

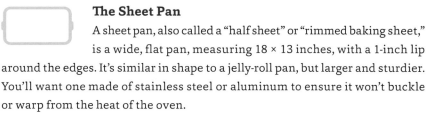

The Sheet Pan
A sheet pan, also called a "half sheet" or "rimmed baking sheet," is a wide, flat pan, measuring 18 × 13 inches, with a 1-inch lip around the edges. It's similar in shape to a jelly-roll pan, but larger and sturdier. You'll want one made of stainless steel or aluminum to ensure it won't buckle or warp from the heat of the oven.

The true beauty of the sheet pan lies in its large surface area and shallow sides, which allow the hot air from your oven to really circulate around whatever's cooking, drawing out moisture and producing extra-crispy chicken skin, succulent veggies, or perfectly browned cake corners. Not only are sheet pans true workhorses in the kitchen (helpful for everything from broiling trays of meat to big-batch baking), but they're also inexpensive and easy to find. Plus, lining your sheet pans with foil or parchment paper makes cleanup the easiest. I recommend owning at least two.

A few of my sheet pan recipes will call for a wire rack to be set on top of the pan. This fun trick doubles the pan surface (we can roast chicken on the rack and broccoli below, let's say) and imparts lots of flavor to the finished dish (broccoli flavored with chicken drippings, yum). It also doubles as a cooling rack for baked goods! You probably already have a wire rack in your cupboard, but if you don't, look for a sturdy metal one that's ovenproof.

The Cast Iron Skillet

One of the most durable and reliable pieces of kitchen equipment in the bunch, a cast iron skillet is the kind of pan that gets passed down from generation to generation, its seasoned patina building up over time and holding memories of meals long past, like Great-Grandma's fried chicken, Dad's sticky cinnamon rolls, or your aunt's famous stuffed cabbage. I love a cast iron skillet for its ability to hold heat like crazy and to move seamlessly from the stovetop to the oven, which means we can get a nice sear on the meat (or fish, veggies, what have you) before finishing our meal, hands-free, in the oven. Even if you don't have one that's been passed down for generations, it's easy (and cheap) to procure a good one that'll last you forever—Lodge makes a great, preseasoned cast iron skillet that'll only set you back about sixteen bucks—and for the recipes in this book, a classic, 10-inch skillet is the way to go. (If you don't have a 10-inch skillet, err on the bigger-is-better side, and use a 12-inch instead. Alternatively, you can use your favorite, non–cast iron pan; just make sure it's oven-safe.)

There's a lot of confusion and uncertainty around how to "season," maintain, and clean cast iron, but in truth there's not much to it. If you've inherited a very old pan, odds are it's had years to build up a lovely patina or coating, which just means that it's absorbed years' worth of cooking oil and as a result has become naturally nonstick. If your pan is brand-new, even if it's been marketed as preseasoned, you'll want to build up your own nonstick coating over time. Start by washing the pan with hot, soapy water and then drying it thoroughly (moisture is the enemy of cast iron, which can rust if not dried properly). Rub the pan all over with corn, vegetable, or canola oil, using a paper towel to reach all of the nooks and crannies, and then place the pan in a 450°F oven for 30 minutes. (It will smoke.) Repeat the oiling and heating steps three or four times (all at once or over a few days, if you like), then let the pan cool completely on the stovetop (it will look much blacker than it was when you started). Voilà! You've just seasoned your first cast iron skillet.

To maintain your seasoned pan, use it regularly, and clean it immediately after using with a bit of dish soap and a soft sponge (never soak it, which, again, can lead to rusting). Dry your skillet well—I often put my cleaned skillet back on a hot burner to help it dry completely—and apply a thin coating of oil before storing it.

There you have it! Now, was that so terrible? Just remember, when it comes to taking care of cast iron, moisture is bad and (corn, vegetable, or canola) oil is good. With proper love and care, you'll be passing your trusty seasoned skillet down to your children's children, along with your recipe for Artichoke Gratin (page 65).

The Dutch Oven

I feel like sonnets and odes should be written to the Dutch oven— what usefulness, what range, what absolute versatility! Plus, it can be really pretty. A deep, lidded pot made of stainless steel or heavy cast iron and often coated in enamel, a Dutch oven can braise, bake, and simmer stews with the best of them. It bounces easily from the stovetop to the oven, holding heat beautifully and turning out everything from perfectly tender pulled pork to brothy mussels, from meaty chili to loaded ramen noodle soup (all of which are included in the following pages, by the way).

Dutch ovens can be quite pricey, ranging anywhere from $50 to over $300 for a nice Staub or Le Creuset, but when it comes to these pots, price is generally a trustworthy indicator of quality. A good one will have a heavy bottom and thick walls, sturdy and graspable handles, and a weighty, well-fitting lid. I'd start with a 5- to 6-quart Dutch oven, which will work perfectly for most of the recipes herein, but if you're looking to fully outfit yourself (and cook for large crowds, say), I'd get a larger, 7- to 8-quart pot, too, which a handful of the recipes here do call for. They're an investment, to be sure, but much like your cast iron skillet, your Dutch oven will stand the test of time and last you pretty much forever.

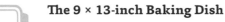

The 9 × 13-inch Baking Dish

Ah, the trusty casserole dish, as tried and true as Mom's famous lasagna. A 9 × 13-inch pan is fantastic for when you want a layered, baked dish, usually involving some kind of liquid or sauce, like Pesto Zoodle Casserole (page 90), for example.

There are a number of brands out there, some touting different shapes and materials, but all will work just as well for the recipes in this book. Whether you choose an oval baking dish or a rectangular glass number, just make sure the sides are at least 2 inches tall and the dish can handle 3 quarts of volume. I'm a big fan of the classic glass Pyrex, which is inexpensive and fairly sturdy. The glass dish lets you see exactly how your fish fillets or cookie bars are baking up, and goes easily from the fridge to the oven to the dishwasher for easy cleanup.

The Muffin Tin

Though it's difficult (but not impossible) to build a full meal in a muffin tin, we'll use this pan a lot in the brunch, starters/snacks/sides, and dessert chapters. Muffin tins are fabulous for turning out smaller, individually portioned treats like baked eggs, oatmeal, and brownie cups. I like to use a nonstick metal 12-cup standard muffin tin, which holds up well in the oven and is easy to clean. There are a number of good brands out there, such as Wilton, OXO, and Norpro, which sell for well under twenty dollars. Even with a nonstick pan, I like to grease my muffin tin liberally with butter or olive oil spray to ensure maximum nonstickiness, although paper cupcake liners (or parchment paper squares, which are great improv liners) are a useful and small investment toward that goal, too.

Cake, Pie, Tart, Loaf, and Bundt Pans

CAKE, PIE, OR TART

LOAF

BUNDT

A few other pans that I like to have in my kitchen arsenal (and that we'll use on occasion in this book) include a classic 9-inch round cake pan, an 8-inch square pan, a standard (12-cup) aluminum Bundt pan, a 9 × 5 × 3-inch standard loaf pan, and a 9-inch pie dish or tart pan. I like a nonstick coating on my cake and Bundt pans, which is helpful for turning out perfect treats. And as pie dishes go, I'm fond of regular old glass or ceramic dishes (although glass is more helpful in the "checking for doneness" stage of cooking). We'll use these guys only occasionally in this book, so if you're just looking to shore up on the heavy hitters, come back for these later.

While all of the recipes here cook in just one pan, and I've streamlined the prep and cooking processes for you as much as possible, we'll often dirty a bowl or two in our prep work—but a quick rinse or spin in the dishwasher takes care of those. And occasionally (particularly in the dessert chapter), I'll call for the use of a food processor, blender, or electric mixer—these recipes are noted as One Pan Plus (+). Although hauling out this equipment to make a one pan dish might seem counterintuitive, we'll do it only when it bumps up the recipe's level of ease exponentially. For example, you *could* finely chop the ingredients to make pesto by hand, but why put yourself through that slog when fresh pesto comes together in mere seconds in the food processor? One Pan Plus recipes make use of such helpful equipment to avoid whipping eggs, creaming batter, and finely chopping ingredients by hand. (Though if you're looking for a good arm workout, go ahead and make the Confetti Pavlova, page 228, without a mixer! Triceps of steel, straight ahead.) At their heart, all of the recipes in *One Pan & Done* have you (and your precious hands-on time) in mind. And in the end? We'll have dinner, at least. And if you have leftovers, I'll even tell you how to store and reheat them.

So there you have it! A one pan wonderful party. Let's stock our pantries and get cooking!

• PANTRY TALK •

A quick word on ingredients, because we'll want to stock our kitchens for success. Here's a down-and-dirty list of what I always have on hand in the pantry, and I recommend you have, too.

- **EXTRA VIRGIN OLIVE OIL** The backbone of most dishes, I keep jugs of this stuff at the ready! Extra virgin olive oil is tastier and less refined than other kinds, and generally of a higher quality, although you can still find inexpensive bottles at the grocery store. I like to use the big, lower-priced bottles of extra virgin olive oil for cooking, and keep a smaller, pricier bottle on hand for drizzling on salads and other (uncooked) applications.

- **KOSHER SALT** This is my go-to cooking salt (I like Diamond Crystal). It's flakier and cleaner tasting than other kinds of salt (such as table salt or fine sea salt) and, I find, perfect for most uses in the kitchen. When I call for salt in the recipes in this book, unless otherwise specified, I'm always talking kosher salt. If you use a different kind, you'll want to reduce the amount of salt called for, since kosher salt is less dense than other salts and, therefore, less salty tasting.

- **VINEGAR** I recommend having at least three kinds of vinegar in your pantry: apple cider, balsamic, and rice. I find vinegars quite versatile and interchangeable in general, and with these three you'll be able to whip up most kinds of sauces and dressings, or add a little zip to a one-note pot of soup. If you want to expand your collection, you can't go wrong with a bottle of white wine vinegar, too.

- **LEMONS** Fresh lemons help us take dishes from flat to fantastic, since a splash of lemon juice is often the difference between a pan of seafood that's just "meh" and one that's just marvelous. They help us brighten up all kinds of soups, sauces, dressings, and stews, so I like to make sure we've always got a lemon or two available (and in a pinch, bottled lemon juice will do).

- **SOY SAUCE** I always keep a bottle of soy sauce in my cabinet for whipping up quick, flavorful sauces and marinades. Its briny, umami-flavored bite can't be beat and adds an element of depth to our dishes. The less-sodium version is plenty salty, and that's what I always call for in these recipes.

- **ALL-PURPOSE FLOUR** Though I'll occasionally call for other kinds of flour, particularly in the dessert chapter (such as cake flour, for example), all-purpose flour is just that—all-purpose—and can usually be substituted successfully in most recipes. I keep mine in a large, airtight canister in my pantry, which helps keep it fresh and pure. It's important to aerate your flour before measuring it out, so just stir and fluff it up a bit (with a spoon or measuring cup) before scooping and measuring, which will ensure you get the right amount called for.

- **CANNED BEANS AND DICED TOMATOES** I like to have a few different kinds of canned beans in the cupboard at all times, since they're cheap, highly shelf-stable, and hearty. They can even make a meal in a pinch. A can of chickpeas can turn half of a roasted butternut squash into a respectable dinner, and having a few cans of black beans, kidney beans, or pinto beans, plus a can or two of diced tomatoes, at the ready means that, at any given time, I'm that much closer to getting a warming bowl of chili on the table—and quickly.

- **CHICKEN BROTH** Though you can't beat homemade chicken broth, sometimes time (and life, in general) gets the better of us, and that's okay. I always keep a few boxes of low-sodium chicken and vegetable broth in my pantry, to help round out quick soups, stews, and pan sauces. If I ever have any boxed broth

left over at the end of cooking, I like to freeze it in an ice cube tray so I have a few smaller-portioned bits of broth that are easily thawable and will keep for months.

- **PANKO BREAD CRUMBS** I use panko bread crumbs—which are lighter, airier, and crispier than regular bread crumbs—quite a bit in this book, often to form a crunchy baked coating on meat or vegetables, or to give a casserole a satisfyingly crispy topping. A box of plain panko lasts for a while in the pantry, so I like to always have one on hand.

- **DRIED HERBS AND SPICES** I have a plethora of constantly rotating herbs and spices on my spice rack, but if you're just starting out in the kitchen, the staples I'd recommend picking up are: black peppercorns, dried oregano, paprika, crushed red pepper, ground cumin, ground cinnamon, curry powder, chili powder, nutmeg, and garlic powder. This varied and flavorful mix should see you through most recipes ahead.

- **CHOCOLATE** This one might not be quite as necessary as far as true pantry staples go, but I actually tend to panic if I don't have any chocolate in the cupboard. I like to keep a few bars of unsweetened chocolate for baking, plus a few bags of good bittersweet and semisweet chocolate chips (for baking and snacking) at the ready at all times. Take or leave this information as you will.

And in my fridge? You can always find large eggs and plenty of unsalted butter—I recommend following suit.

All right, that just about covers it all. Easy-peasy, right? Now that we know what we're working with, let's get cooking.

CHAPTER ONE

BREAKFAST & BRUNCH

Herby Egg & Blue Cheese Soufflés 22
Ham & Egg Cups 24
Baked Oatmeal on the Go 44
Warm Buttermilk Doughnut Muffins ➕ 47
Fresh Berry Cornmeal Muffins 49

Cinnamon Toast Bread Pudding 37
Bacon Biscuit Bread 38
Oat & Date Breakfast Bars ➕ 46

Skillet Strata 27
Artichoke Shakshuka 28
Nutty Sticky Rolls 33

Lemon Lavender Pull-Apart Loaf 31

Egg & Goat Cheese Portobello Caps 25
Sweet Potato & Sausage Breakfast Hash 39
Green Bean & Prosciutto Baked Eggs 40

Radish & Ricotta Frittata 43

Orange Sugar Monkey Bread 50

HERBY
EGG &
BLUE CHEESE
SOUFFLÉS

◇ **MAKES 12 SOUFFLÉS** ◇

TANGY BLUE CHEESE AND PLENTY OF FRESH herbs keep these light, simple soufflés on their toes—though if you're not a blue cheese person, crumbled feta or Parmesan could happily stand in. I love that these do equally well as festive brunch fare and quick, weekday breakfast—if you make a batch on Sunday and store the leftovers in the fridge, you'll have easily grabable egg cups all week long.

6 teaspoons extra virgin olive or vegetable oil

12 large eggs

¼ cup milk (not skim)

Kosher salt and ground black pepper

4 ounces crumbled blue cheese (about 1 cup)

¼ cup chopped fresh flat-leaf parsley

1 tablespoon chopped fresh thyme leaves

1 tablespoon chopped fresh dill

¼ cup chopped fresh chives

1   Preheat the oven to 350°F, with a rack in the center position. Pour ½ teaspoon of the oil into each cup of a 12-cup muffin tin. Place the oiled tin in the oven to preheat for 10 minutes.

2   Meanwhile, in a large bowl, whisk together the eggs, milk, and a pinch each of salt and pepper.

3   Carefully remove the pan from the oven and evenly distribute the blue cheese and fresh herbs among the muffin cups. Pour in the egg mixture, filling each cup evenly. Return to the oven and bake until puffed and just starting to brown on top, 15 to 18 minutes.

4   Allow the soufflés to cool for 5 to 10 minutes (they will fall) before turning them out onto a cutting board and serving either warm or at room temperature.

5   The egg soufflés will keep, in an airtight container, for 4 to 5 days in the refrigerator. Microwave for 30 seconds to 1 minute each to rewarm.

HAM & EGG
CUPS

> MAKES 12 EGG CUPS

BACON AND EGGS, ALL IN ONE NEAT LITTLE package! Breakfast brilliance. I like adding some punch with diced green chiles, sharp cheddar, and tangy scallions, though you should feel free to swap out the add-ins to your liking. Maybe chopped olives, feta, and dried oregano sounds more your speed if you're going Greek. Or a dollop of Dijon and some Gruyère? *Oui.* Just don't leave out the bacon, because . . . well, bacon.

12 slices Canadian bacon

6 tablespoons canned diced green chiles

12 large eggs

½ cup shredded sharp cheddar cheese

2 scallions, white and light green parts only, chopped

Kosher salt and ground black pepper

1 Preheat the oven to 350°F, with a rack in the center position. Grease a standard 12-cup muffin tin with butter or cooking spray.

2 Tuck a slice of Canadian bacon into each muffin cup, forming a little cup. Transfer the pan to the oven and bake until some of the fat has rendered and the bacon just starts to brown, about 10 minutes.

3 Remove the pan from the oven and fill each bacon "cup" with ½ tablespoon of the diced green chiles, 1 egg, a sprinkle of cheddar, some chopped scallion, and a pinch each of kosher salt and pepper. Return the pan to the oven and bake until the egg whites have set but the yolks are still a bit runny, 10 to 15 minutes.

4 Allow the pan to cool for 10 minutes, then carefully pop the ham-and-egg cups from the muffin tin with the help of a paring knife or small offset spatula. Serve warm.

HOW TO?
CRACK EGGS CLEANLY

I find the best way to crack eggs is to give them a quick rap on a flat surface (the countertop, usually), then gently break them open with my thumbs. This method prevents jagged pieces of shell from piercing the yolks (which can easily happen if you try cracking them on the side of a bowl) and keeps the eggs intact.

EGG & GOAT CHEESE PORTOBELLO CAPS

> SERVES 6 TO 8

HERE, MEATY PORTOBELLO MUSHROOM CAPS make the perfect bed for baked eggs sprinkled with creamy goat cheese and fresh herbs. If your portobellos don't have much of a curved, "cuppish" shape, the eggs may slide off when you try to nestle them in there, but not to worry—they taste just as good either way.

8 large portobello mushroom caps

2 tablespoons extra virgin olive oil

Kosher salt and ground black pepper

8 large eggs

½ cup crumbled goat cheese

2 teaspoons chopped fresh thyme leaves

1 tablespoon chopped fresh dill

1 Preheat the oven to 400°F, with a rack in the center position. Line a sheet pan with foil and mist with cooking spray.

2 Gently scoop out the black gills of the mushrooms and discard. Drizzle the inside of the caps with the olive oil and a pinch of kosher salt and arrange them, scooped-side down, on the prepared sheet pan. Transfer to the oven and roast until tender, 10 to 15 minutes.

3 Remove from the oven and flip the mushrooms scooped-side up. Crack an egg (see tip, opposite) into each mushroom cup and sprinkle with goat cheese, thyme, and a pinch each of salt and pepper. Return the pan to the oven and bake until the egg whites are set but the yolks are still a bit runny, 10 to 15 minutes.

4 Top the yolks with fresh dill and serve the egg caps warm.

SKILLET STRATA

WHAT EXACTLY IS A STRATA? JUST A breakfast casserole of the highest order! This one's got it all—caramelized onions, sautéed mushrooms, hearty bread cubes, shredded cheese, fresh herbs, and maple sausage, all held together by a savory egg custard. It's real-deal delicious. And here's a pro tip: To get a jump on this the night before brunch, sauté the sausage, onion, and mushrooms in the pan, then let everything cool before adding the bread cubes and egg mixture and letting the whole thing soak and meld (well wrapped, in the refrigerator) overnight. Then just bake off the strata the next morning! (And watch your guests trip over themselves for seconds . . .)

2 tablespoons extra virgin olive oil

4 links maple breakfast sausage (about 12 ounces), cut into ½-inch-thick slices

1 small onion, thinly sliced

2 cups sliced cremini mushrooms

6 large eggs

1 cup whole milk or half-and-half

1½ tablespoons Dijon mustard

2 tablespoons chopped fresh chives, plus more for topping

Kosher salt and ground black pepper

4 cups 1-inch bread cubes (I like to use ciabatta or a baguette)

1½ cups shredded Gruyère cheese (about 6 ounces)

1 Preheat the oven to 400°F, with a rack in the center position.

2 Heat the olive oil in a 10-inch cast iron skillet over medium-high heat. When the oil is shimmering, add the sausage and sauté until well browned and cooked through. Stir in the onion and mushrooms, and continue cooking until the vegetables begin to soften and brown, about 7 minutes.

3 While the sausage and vegetables cook, in a large bowl, whisk together the eggs, milk, mustard, chives, and a big pinch each of salt and pepper.

4 Add the cubed bread to the skillet in a single layer and top with the Gruyère. Remove from the heat and pour the egg mixture over the bread, distributing it evenly around the pan. Gently press the bread down with a spoon to help it soak up the egg mixture.

5 Transfer the skillet to the oven and bake until the strata is browned, puffed, and set, 25 to 30 minutes.

6 Sprinkle more chopped chives over the strata and serve it warm from the skillet, family-style.

ARTICHOKE
SHAKSHUKA

> SERVES 4

IF YOU'RE EVER INVITED TO MY SISTER'S HOUSE for a meal (and I don't know why you wouldn't be, she definitely likes you), whether breakfast, lunch, or dinner, odds are you'll sit down to a steaming pan of Casey's famous *shakshuka*. It was her idea to add briny, bright artichokes to this simple, satisfying dish, and I'm convinced that this is exactly where artichokes belong. As Casey says, this dish is great for guests because it "looks super fancy," and all you need to serve it with is a loaf of crusty bread for scooping up the extra sauce, but it's also the perfect, hands-off meal to make for yourself, "because you matter." So true, Casey, so true.

2 tablespoons extra virgin olive oil

1 small yellow onion, thinly sliced

1 red bell pepper, thinly sliced

1 (24-ounce) jar good marinara sauce (I like Rao's)

1 (12-ounce) jar marinated artichoke hearts, drained and quartered

6 to 8 large eggs

Kosher salt and ground black pepper

1 cup crumbled feta or goat cheese (about 4 ounces)

2 tablespoons chopped fresh flat-leaf parsley

1 Preheat the oven to 375°F, with a rack in the center position.

2 Heat the olive oil in a 10-inch cast iron skillet over medium-high heat. When the oil is shimmering, add the onion and bell pepper and sauté until just beginning to soften, about 5 minutes.

3 Remove the pan from the heat and add the marinara and artichoke hearts. Crack the eggs into the sauce (for tip, see page 24) and sprinkle each with a generous pinch each of salt and black pepper. Sprinkle the crumbled cheese over the pan.

4 Transfer the pan to the oven and bake until the egg whites are set but the yolks are still a bit runny, 15 to 20 minutes.

5 Scatter the fresh parsley over the pan before serving warm from the skillet, family-style.

LEMON LAVENDER PULL-APART LOAF

∘⟨ **SERVES 4 TO 6** ⟩∘

THIS LEMONY, NOT-TOO-SWEET BREAKFAST bread is meant for sharing. Making the dough from scratch is fun and rewarding, and I've given you instructions to do so if you'd like, but there's nothing wrong with using store-bought, if that's more your speed. Either way, please invite me over for brunch. I'm very good at helping "even out" the jagged edges of pull-apart bread, you see. In the name of being helpful.

2 tablespoons grated lemon zest (from about 2 lemons)

2 teaspoons dried lavender buds

½ cup sugar

2 (8-ounce) cans store-bought refrigerated buttermilk biscuit dough, or homemade dough (see page 32)

4 tablespoons unsalted butter, melted

1 Preheat the oven to 350°F, with a rack in the center position. Grease and flour a standard loaf pan.

2 In a medium bowl, use the tips of your fingers to work the lemon zest and dried lavender into the sugar, rubbing everything together until the sugar is brightly colored and fragrant.

3 Remove the biscuits from the package and roll each one out into a flat round about ½ inch thick. Lightly brush the rounds with the melted butter and sprinkle a scant teaspoon of the lemon-lavender sugar on top of each, using your fingers to spread it evenly around. Fold the round of dough in half, then arrange the half-moons of dough tightly in the prepared loaf pan, laying the flat edges on the bottom of the pan, with the rounded edges pointing up. Brush any remaining melted butter on top of the loaf, and sprinkle over any extra sugar.

4 Transfer the pan to the oven and bake until deeply golden all over and a thermometer inserted into the center reads at least 200°F, 30 to 35 minutes.

5 Allow the bread to cool in the pan for 30 minutes, then run a paring knife around the sides to loosen the loaf before carefully inverting onto a cutting board. Gently place a plate or serving platter on top of the inverted loaf, then flip carefully to set right side up.

6 Enjoy it warm. Bread is best the day it's made, but can be tightly wrapped and stored at room temperature for about 2 days. Rewarm in the microwave or a 275°F oven to refresh before serving.

DIY DOUGH!

IF YOU WANT TO MAKE THE DOUGH FROM scratch, here's how:

2¾ cups plus 2 tablespoons all-purpose flour

¼ cup sugar

2¼ teaspoons (1 envelope) rapid-rise yeast

½ teaspoon kosher salt

4 tablespoons unsalted butter

⅓ cup whole milk

¼ cup water

1 teaspoon pure vanilla extract

2 large eggs, at room temperature, lightly beaten

1 In a large bowl, whisk together 2 cups of the flour, the sugar, yeast, and salt.

2 Melt the butter into the milk, either in a small saucepan over medium heat or in 15-second increments in the microwave. Add the water and vanilla and stir to help it cool down.

3 When the milk mixture has cooled to be just warm to the touch, pour it over the flour mixture and stir to incorporate. Add the eggs and continue stirring until combined. Add an additional ¾ cup flour and stir until a somewhat sticky dough comes together.

4 Transfer the dough to a large, well-oiled bowl and cover it with a clean kitchen towel. Place the bowl in a warm corner of the kitchen and let it rise until doubled in size, 30 minutes to 1 hour. (Note: If you want to break up this process, you can let the dough rise in the refrigerator overnight, covered with plastic wrap.)

5 When the dough has risen, turn it out onto a lightly floured surface. Work another 2 tablespoons of flour into it until it's nice and smooth. Cover it with your clean kitchen towel and let it rest for 5 minutes.

6 When the dough has rested, roll it into a roughly 12 × 20-inch rectangle. Brush the dough with melted butter and sprinkle the lemon lavender sugar evenly on top, pressing gently to adhere.

7 Use a sharp knife to cut the dough lengthwise into 6 strips of equal width. Stack the strips on top of one another and then cut the stack crosswise into 6 pieces (you'll end up with 6 square stacks of dough).

8 Arrange the dough stacks sideways in the prepared loaf pan—the sugared sides will face the ends of the loaf pan, and the cut edges of the dough will stand up straight like the pages of a book. Cover the pan with a clean kitchen towel and let the dough rise once more, until nearly doubled in size, 20 to 30 minutes. Then just proceed with the recipe as written.

NUTTY STICKY ROLLS

>< MAKES 12 ROLLS ><

FOR WHEN YOU NEED STICKY ROLLS ON THE quick! There's no yeast involved in these gooey, nutty delights, so there's no need to bother with the proof, the rise, the agonizing WAIT for warm, caramely morning buns. The rolls come out of the oven soft and tantalizingly sticky, but they firm up quickly, so plan to serve them immediately after baking.

FOR THE CARAMEL

4 tablespoons unsalted butter

½ cup packed dark brown sugar

½ cup heavy cream

2 tablespoons pure maple syrup

¾ teaspoon kosher salt

FOR THE DOUGH

3 cups all-purpose flour, plus more for rolling the dough

2 tablespoons granulated sugar

1¼ teaspoons baking powder

½ teaspoon baking soda

½ teaspoon kosher salt

1 cup buttermilk, at room temperature

1 teaspoon pure vanilla extract

4 tablespoons unsalted butter, melted

FOR THE FILLING

½ cup packed dark brown sugar

½ teaspoon ground cinnamon

¼ teaspoon ground cardamom

½ cup roughly chopped pecans

1   Preheat the oven to 400°F, with a rack in the center position.

2   To make the caramel: Melt the butter in a 10-inch cast iron skillet over medium heat. Add the brown sugar, cream, maple syrup, and salt and whisk to combine. Bring to a boil, simmer for 1 minute, then remove from the heat and allow the caramel to cool down while you make the dough.

3   To make the dough: In a large bowl, whisk together the flour, granulated sugar, baking powder, baking soda, and salt. Pour in the buttermilk, vanilla, and melted butter and stir to combine until a shaggy dough forms.

RECIPE CONTINUES

4 Turn the dough out onto a well-floured surface and knead it gently a few times, just to smooth it out. Use a well-floured rolling pin to roll the dough into a 9 × 12-inch rectangle, with the longer side facing you.

5 To make the filling: In a small bowl, stir together the brown sugar, cinnamon, and cardamom.

6 Gently brush the rectangle of dough with water and sprinkle the filling evenly over the dough, pressing lightly to adhere. Working from the top edge (the long side farthest from you) down, roll the dough into a tight log, pinching the seam closed as best you can. Use a serrated knife to gently slice the log crosswise into twelve 1-inch pieces.

7 Scatter the chopped pecans over the cooled caramel in the skillet, then tuck the cinnamony buns, cut-side up, over the nutty topping, arranging them evenly in the pan (squeeze them tightly together to fit, if necessary).

8 Slide the pan into the oven and bake until the rolls are golden brown and the topping is bubbling, 25 to 30 minutes. You may want to stick a piece of foil or a sheet pan underneath the cast iron, to catch any errant drips of caramel.

9 When the buns are deeply golden, remove the pan from the oven and immediately, but carefully, invert the skillet onto a serving platter. Let the inverted skillet sit for about 20 seconds before lifting up to release the buns. Scrape down any caramel topping stuck to the pan and pile it on top of the sticky buns.

10 Enjoy warm. If the buns sit too long and start to harden, simply rewarm in the microwave, or cover with foil and reheat in a 350°F oven for 10 minutes.

CINNAMON TOAST
BREAD
PUDDING

⤝ **SERVES 6 TO 8** ⤞

THIS DISH IS ONE OF MY FAVORITE THINGS TO serve when I have company for brunch because it looks beautifully decadent (come to think of it, it tastes beautifully decadent, too) but takes just minutes to prep and, best of all, can be assembled the night before. And it's so easily customizable! Swap vanilla or almond for coffee extract, throw in some citrus zest, add berries, raisins, or other dried fruit—this pudding takes it all in stride. Just make sure to serve with a splash of maple syrup, a dusting of powdered sugar, or some sugared berries alongside.

16 (1-inch-thick) slices cinnamon swirl bread (about 1½ loaves)

2 cups milk (not skim)

1 cup heavy cream

6 large eggs

1¼ teaspoons ground cinnamon

½ teaspoon kosher salt

1 teaspoon coffee liqueur or extract

1 tablespoon molasses

⅓ cup pure maple syrup, plus more for serving

¼ cup packed light brown sugar

1   The night before serving, mist a 9 × 13-inch pan with cooking spray. Arrange the bread in overlapping slices in the prepared pan, packing them fairly tightly.

2   In a large bowl, whisk together the milk, cream, eggs, ¼ teaspoon of the cinnamon, the salt, coffee liqueur, molasses, and maple syrup until smooth. Pour the custard over the bread, letting it soak into each piece. Cover the dish with foil and allow to rest in the refrigerator overnight.

3   When ready to bake, preheat the oven to 350°F, with a rack in the center position.

4   Remove the soaked bread from the refrigerator. In a small bowl, whisk together the brown sugar and remaining 1 teaspoon cinnamon. Sprinkle the cinnamon sugar evenly over the dish.

5   Transfer the dish to the oven and bake until the bread pudding is very well browned and jiggles only slightly in the center, 45 minutes to 1 hour.

6   Allow the dish to cool slightly before serving warm, with extra maple syrup if you like. (I do.)

BACON BISCUIT BREAD

THIS IS BASICALLY A BATCH OF FLUFFY buttermilk biscuits in bread form—baked over a bed of crispy bacon, that is. It is baked as a whole loaf, so we don't need to bother with cutting or shaping individual biscuits, but we'll still get richly risen, buttery biscuit flavor, with a salty, bacony bite thrown in for good measure. Drizzled with sweet, sticky honey on top, this bread is what brunch dreams are made of.

3 slices thick-cut bacon, cut into ½-inch-wide pieces

3 cups all-purpose flour

¼ cup sugar

1 tablespoon baking powder

1 teaspoon baking soda

1 teaspoon kosher salt

1 egg, lightly beaten

2 cups buttermilk

4 tablespoons unsalted butter, melted

Butter and honey, for serving (optional)

1 Preheat the oven to 350°F, with a rack in the center position.

2 Scatter the chopped bacon into a 9 × 13-inch baking dish, spreading it evenly around the pan. Bake until the bacon has rendered its fat and is crisp and browned, about 20 minutes.

3 Meanwhile, in a large bowl, stir together the flour, sugar, baking powder, baking soda, and salt until well combined. Add the egg, buttermilk, and melted butter and stir just until the batter comes together.

4 When the bacon is crisp, remove the pan from the oven and pour the batter over the bacon (don't drain any of the ample bacon grease) and spread it evenly to reach the corners of the pan. Return the pan to the oven and bake until the biscuit bread is golden, cracked, and set, about 20 minutes.

5 Allow the bread to cool for 10 minutes before slicing into squares and serving, slathered with extra butter and drizzled with honey, if you like.

SWEET POTATO

& SAUSAGE

BREAKFAST HASH

◇ SERVES 4 TO 6 ◇

SAVORY CHICKEN SAUSAGE PAIRS PERFECTLY here with roasted sweet potatoes and red onion. Topped with fresh eggs, and it all cooks together on one pan? Yes, please. Lining the pan with foil or parchment is the veteran move for the quickest, easiest cleanup you ever did see.

2 medium sweet potatoes, cut into 1-inch cubes

4 links fully cooked chicken apple sausage (I like Applegate), sliced into ½-inch rounds

1 small red onion, cut into ½-inch-thick wedges

3 tablespoons extra virgin olive oil

Kosher salt

8 to 12 large eggs

Crushed red pepper

1   Preheat the oven to 400°F, with a rack in the center position. Line a sheet pan with foil and mist with cooking spray.

2   Toss the sweet potatoes, sausage, and red onion with the olive oil and a generous pinch of salt on the prepared sheet pan and arrange everything in a single layer.

3   Slide into the oven and roast until the sweet potatoes are tender and the sausage is browned, 20 to 30 minutes.

4   Remove the pan from the oven and use a wooden spoon to make 8 to 12 spaces on the pan to accommodate the eggs. Crack an egg into each empty space (see tip, page 24), and sprinkle some salt and a pinch of pepper flakes on top of them.

5   Return the pan to the oven and bake until the egg whites are set but the yolks are still a bit runny, 10 to 15 minutes.

6   Enjoy the breakfast hash warm from the oven.

GREEN BEAN &
PROSCIUTTO
BAKED EGGS

SERVES 4 TO 6

CRISP-TENDER GREEN BEANS AND THIN, SALTY prosciutto slices make a sophisticated nest for softly baked eggs and a sprinkling of fresh Parmesan cheese. It's an Italian-inspired slant on the simplest of brunch dishes (though, honestly, it'd make a fantastic dinner, too). Serve with some toasty, buttered bread for sopping up warm, runny yolks.

2 pounds green beans, ends trimmed

3 tablespoons extra virgin olive oil

8 to 12 thin slices prosciutto

8 to 12 large eggs

Ground black pepper

1 cup grated Parmesan cheese (4 ounces)

1 Preheat the oven to 400°F, with a rack in the center position. Line a sheet pan with foil and mist with cooking spray.

2 Toss the green beans with the olive oil on the prepared pan and spread them in an even layer. Nestle the prosciutto slices among the green beans, creating 8 to 12 little "nests" for the eggs. Crack the eggs into the prosciutto nests (for tip, see page 24) and sprinkle with a pinch of ground black pepper. Scatter the grated Parmesan over the pan.

3 Transfer to the oven and bake until the green beans are crisp-tender and the egg whites are set but the yolks are still a bit runny, 10 to 15 minutes.

RADISH
& RICOTTA
FRITTATA

⊰ **SERVES 6 TO 8** ⊱

FRITTATAS (BASICALLY JUST QUICHES WITHOUT crusts) are almost as much fun to eat as they are to pronounce—plus they're wonderful served either warm or at room temperature, so they're perfect for long, leisurely brunch gatherings. This one boasts the beauty of crisp, thinly sliced radishes and plenty of fresh herbs and cheese, too. It's a sunny celebration of springtime, all in one delicious pan.

1 bunch radishes, thinly sliced, green tops reserved

3 scallions, white and light green parts only, thinly sliced

6 large eggs

Kosher salt and ground black pepper

1 cup whole-milk ricotta cheese

2 ounces herbed goat cheese, crumbled

1 tablespoon chopped fresh tarragon

1 tablespoon chopped fresh chives

1 Preheat the oven to 375°F, with a rack in the center position. Grease a 9-inch pie dish with butter or cooking spray.

2 Arrange the sliced radishes in an even layer in the prepared pie dish and scatter the scallions and a handful of reserved radish tops (roughly chop them, if they're very large) on top.

3 In a large bowl, whisk together the eggs and a generous pinch each of salt and pepper. Stir in the ricotta and carefully pour the egg mixture on top of the radishes, being sure it reaches the edges of the pie dish.

4 Scatter the goat cheese around the pan, and sprinkle the tarragon and chives on top.

5 Transfer the pie dish to the oven and bake until completely set in the center and beginning to brown at the edges, 25 to 30 minutes.

6 Allow to cool before slicing into wedges. Serve warm or at room temperature.

BAKED OATMEAL ON THE GO

MAKES 12

2¼ cups old-fashioned rolled oats

¾ cup toasted, chopped walnuts

1½ teaspoons baking powder

2 teaspoons ground cinnamon

½ teaspoon kosher salt

½ cup pure maple syrup

2 cups milk

2 large eggs

4 tablespoons unsalted butter, melted

1 teaspoon pure vanilla extract

Fresh berries, dried fruit, or extra nuts, for topping (optional)

HERE'S A FUN SOLUTION FOR NOT HAVING enough time to make a fresh batch of oatmeal every morning before work (or school, or parenting, or living the dream, or what have you). Oatmeal baked in muffin cups! The muffins are easily transportable and rewarmable, so you can make a big batch on Sunday and have little portions of oatmeal all week. It's easy to get small kiddos involved in this recipe, too—they'll enjoy topping it with their favorite chopped fruit, nuts, or even a few chocolate chips, if you're that kind of parent (the fun kind, obviously).

1 Preheat the oven to 350°F, with a rack in the center position. Line a 12-cup muffin tin with paper liners.

2 In a large bowl, mix together the oats, nuts, baking powder, cinnamon, and salt. Divide the oat mixture evenly among the lined muffin cups.

3 In a medium bowl, whisk together the maple syrup, milk, eggs, melted butter, and vanilla until smooth. Slowly pour the wet mixture over the oats in the muffin tin, distributing it evenly. Bake until the oatmeal cups are firm and browned on top, 16 to 18 minutes.

4 Allow to cool slightly before popping the oatmeal cups out of the muffin tin.

5 Serve warm or at room temperature. To reheat, put the oatmeal cups in the microwave for 30-second intervals until warm. Store leftovers in the refrigerator for up to a week.

FUN HACK! MUFFIN TIN LINERS Out of muffin tin liners? Small squares of parchment paper make excellent substitutes. (And, bonus, they look pretty cute!) Just roughly cut 4-inch squares of parchment paper and tuck them into the muffin cups, pointy tips upright. They won't look quite as clean as regular paper liners, but that's part of their charm, no?

OAT & DATE BREAKFAST BARS

THESE BREAKFAST BARS BOAST A FORMIDABLE amount of butter, sure, but they're also packed with oats, warm cinnamon, and the natural sweetness of soft, pitted dates. There's some fresh lemon zest and vanilla extract thrown into the mix for good measure. They're pretty much cookies for breakfast, in the best way possible.

1½ cups roughly chopped pitted dates

1 cup boiling water

1 teaspoon grated lemon zest

1 teaspoon pure vanilla extract

1½ cups all-purpose flour

½ cup packed dark brown sugar

1 cup old-fashioned rolled oats

1 teaspoon ground cinnamon

½ teaspoon baking soda

½ teaspoon kosher salt

1½ sticks (6 ounces) unsalted butter, diced

1 Preheat the oven to 350°F, with a rack in the center position. Mist an 8-inch square pan with cooking spray. Line it with parchment paper, leaving a 1-inch overhang on opposite sides, and mist the parchment, too.

2 In a blender or food processor, pulse the dates with the boiling water and lemon zest until a thick, slightly chunky puree is formed. Pulse in the vanilla.

3 In a medium bowl, whisk together the flour, brown sugar, oats, cinnamon, baking soda, and salt. Add the butter and work it in with your fingers until well incorporated and crumbly.

4 Press half of the oat mixture into the bottom of the prepared pan in an even layer. Spread the date paste on top, then evenly distribute the remaining oat mixture over the date paste, and press gently to the edges.

5 Transfer to the oven and bake until the top is crisp and well browned, about 45 minutes.

6 Allow to cool for 20 to 30 minutes before using the parchment overhang to lift the square out of the pan to cool completely. When cool, use a sharp knife to cut into 16 breakfast bars.

7 The bars will last, well wrapped, at room temperature for about a week.

WARM
BUTTERMILK
DOUGHNUT MUFFINS

> MAKES 12 DOUGHNUT MUFFINS

ARE THESE MUFFINS? ARE THEY DOUGHNUTS?
Or some amalgamation of the two?
When you bite into a warm, nutmegy pillow of buttermilk-enriched dough that's
been dipped in melted butter and then
rolled generously in piles of cinnamon
sugar, does it really even matter?

(Update: I'm just getting word that the
answer to that last question is no, no it
doesn't.)

8 tablespoons (1 stick) butter, at room temperature,
   plus more for greasing the pan
¼ cup vegetable oil
1½ cups granulated sugar
⅓ cup packed light brown sugar
2 large eggs
1½ teaspoons baking powder
¼ teaspoon baking soda
1 teaspoon ground nutmeg
1 teaspoon pure vanilla extract
2⅔ cups all-purpose flour
1 cup buttermilk
2 tablespoons ground cinnamon, for rolling

1 Preheat the oven to 425°F, with a rack in the center position. Grease a 12-cup muffin tin with butter or cooking spray.

2 With an electric mixer, cream together 4 tablespoons of the butter with the oil, ½ cup of the granulated sugar, and the brown sugar until smooth and light. Beat in the eggs, one at a time, until combined. Add the baking powder, baking soda, nutmeg, and vanilla, mixing well.

3 Add half of the flour and stir gently to incorporate, then add the buttermilk, and finish by mixing in the rest of the flour just until the batter comes together.

4 Scoop the dough into the prepared muffin cups, filling each almost to the top. Bake until golden brown and a tester inserted into the center of the largest muffin comes out clean, 15 to 17 minutes.

5 Meanwhile, melt the remaining 4 tablespoons butter. In a small bowl, whisk together the remaining 1 cup granulated sugar and the cinnamon.

6 Remove the muffins from the oven and allow to cool for 5 minutes. While still warm, turn them out onto a work surface. Dip each muffin top (and the sides, if you can) in the melted butter, then roll in the cinnamon sugar to thickly coat. The muffins are best enjoyed the day they're made, but you can store them wrapped tightly at room temperature for a day or two.

FRESH BERRY
CORNMEAL
MUFFINS

FULL OF YELLOW CORNMEAL AND FRESH berries, this is my go-to muffin recipe. They're simple to throw together and always crowd-pleasing—the cornmeal provides great structure and chew, and the berries slump into little pockets of fruity goodness throughout. They're perfect on their own, but *sublime* topped with a smear of salted butter.

SUBBING OUT

If you don't have sour cream on hand, feel free to substitute buttermilk or plain Greek yogurt.

1½ cups all-purpose flour

1½ cups yellow cornmeal

¾ cup sugar

2 teaspoons baking powder

1 teaspoon baking soda

1 teaspoon kosher salt

2 large eggs

¾ cup sour cream

¾ cup canola oil

1 teaspoon pure vanilla extract

1½ cups mixed fresh berries, rinsed and well dried

1   Preheat the oven to 375°F, with a rack in the center position. Line a 12-cup muffin tin with paper liners and mist the top of the pan with cooking spray.

2   In a large bowl, stir together the flour, cornmeal, sugar, baking powder, baking soda, and salt until combined.

3   In another large bowl, whisk together the eggs, sour cream, canola oil, and vanilla until smooth. Add the dry ingredients to the wet and mix gently until the batter just comes together. Fold in the berries.

4   Divide the batter among the prepared muffin cups, so each is just over three-fourths full. Transfer to the oven and bake until a tester inserted into the center of the largest muffin comes out clean, 25 to 30 minutes.

5   Allow the muffins to cool for 5 minutes before turning them out of the pan. Muffins are best served warm from the oven.

ORANGE SUGAR MONKEY BREAD

⊱ SERVES 6 TO 8 ⊰

WANT TO INTRODUCE ONE SET OF FRIENDS TO another? Ensure the in-laws get along? Or break the ice at your awkward office party? Serve monkey bread. Sharing monkey bread makes everyone friends! Aside from the fact that eating it forces people to (literally) break bread together, there's just nothing awkward or unfriendly about warm, sweet bread, sticky with caramelized sugar and heavily infused with fresh orange.

8 tablespoons (1 stick) unsalted butter, melted and cooled, plus more for greasing the pan

2 tablespoons grated orange zest

1 cup sugar

2 (8-ounce) cans store-bought refrigerated buttermilk biscuit dough, biscuits quartered, or homemade dough (see page 72)

Chopped pistachios, for topping (optional)

1 Preheat the oven to 350°F. Grease a 12-cup Bundt pan with butter or cooking spray.

2 Pour the melted butter into a small bowl. In a medium bowl, use the tips of your fingers to work the orange zest into the sugar until the sugar is fragrant and yellowish-orange.

3 Dunk each piece of dough into the melted butter, then roll it in the orange-sugar mixture. Place the coated dough balls in the prepared Bundt pan, spacing them about ½ inch apart and creating layers. When the dough has been used up, mix any remaining butter and orange sugar together and pour it over the dough in the pan.

4 Transfer the Bundt pan to the oven and bake until the monkey bread is fragrant and golden brown, with a dark, sugary crust, 30 to 40 minutes.

5 Let the bread cool in the pan for about 15 minutes before carefully inverting it onto a large plate or serving platter. Top with chopped pistachios, if you like. The cake is best served warm.

CHAPTER TWO

STARTERS, SNACKS & SIDES

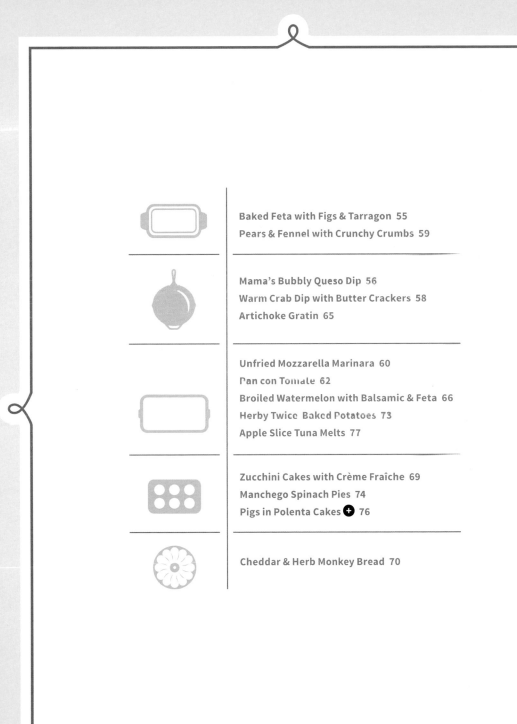

Baked Feta with Figs & Tarragon 55
Pears & Fennel with Crunchy Crumbs 59

Mama's Bubbly Queso Dip 56
Warm Crab Dip with Butter Crackers 58
Artichoke Gratin 65

Unfried Mozzarella Marinara 60
Pan con Tomate 62
Broiled Watermelon with Balsamic & Feta 66
Herby Twice Baked Potatoes 73
Apple Slice Tuna Melts 77

Zucchini Cakes with Crème Fraîche 69
Manchego Spinach Pies 74
Pigs in Polenta Cakes ➕ 76

Cheddar & Herb Monkey Bread 70

BAKED FETA

WITH

FIGS & TARRAGON

⊱ SERVES 4 TO 6 ⊰

SWEET, DELICATE, AND ONLY AROUND FOR A short season, fresh figs feel like fruit royalty, and I'm usually quite happy to eat them straight from the container—the sweet, soft flesh yielding easily, the tiny seeds popping gently between my teeth. But, perfect as they are on their own, I find that they reach sublime status when paired with warm feta, a drizzle of honey, and fresh tarragon. This is one of the easiest and most beautiful appetizers out there, so go! Scoop up those figs! (And if fig season eludes you, feel free to substitute fresh blackberries or sliced plums instead.)

¾ pound fresh figs (about 12), halved lengthwise
2 tablespoons extra virgin olive oil
½ teaspoon kosher salt
Pinch of ground black pepper
1 (8-ounce) block feta cheese
1 teaspoon honey
1 tablespoon roughly chopped fresh tarragon
Assorted crackers, for serving

1   Preheat the oven to 375°F, with a rack in the center position.

2   Combine the figs in a 9 × 13-inch baking dish with 1 tablespoon of the olive oil, the salt, and pepper and toss to coat. Nudge the figs toward the edges of the baking dish, and place the block of feta in the center.

3   Drizzle the remaining 1 tablespoon olive oil and the honey over the cheese, then sprinkle the tarragon over the entire dish.

4   Transfer the dish to the oven and bake until the figs have released some of their juices and the feta is knife-tender, 15 to 20 minutes.

5   Serve warm, with plenty of crackers alongside.

MAMA'S
BUBBLY
QUESO DIP

SERVES 6

EVERY YEAR AROUND THANKSGIVING, MY parents throw a "leftovers party." Leftovers is a loose term—we usually end up cooking an entirely new meal, with dishes that have very little to do with traditional Thanksgiving fare—but whatever, that's what it's called. So every year, my mom fills her fondue pot with a jar of store-bought salsa and a giant block of highly processed, bright orange "cheese"…and it's delicious. But I wanted to re-create this childhood memory with fresh ingredients, and bring it into the (wonderfully rich and melty) realm of *real* cheese. It still comes together quickly in one pot, and—dare I say?—it might even be better than the original.

4 plum tomatoes, finely chopped

½ medium red onion, finely chopped

½ medium jalapeño, seeded and finely chopped

½ red bell pepper, finely chopped

¼ teaspoon kosher salt

¼ teaspoon ground black pepper

1 cup grated Fontina cheese (4 ounces)

½ cup shredded low-moisture mozzarella cheese (part-skim or whole-milk)

½ cup shredded sharp cheddar cheese

¼ cup chopped fresh cilantro

½ lime

Chips, for serving

1 Preheat the oven to 375°F, with a rack in the center position.

2 In a 10-inch cast iron skillet, toss together the tomatoes, onion, jalapeño, bell pepper, salt, and black pepper. Layer the cheeses on top, transfer to the oven, and bake until the cheeses are melted and bubbling, about 10 minutes.

3 Top the skillet with a sprinkle of cilantro and a generous squeeze of fresh lime juice, and serve immediately, with plenty of chips alongside for scooping.

WARM CRAB DIP

WITH

BUTTER CRACKERS

SERVES 6

HERE'S A HOT, COMFORTING SKILLET FULL OF indulgence for when you're feeling crabby. (See what I did there?) I don't know why, but crabmeat and cream cheese just seem to belong together in this world. We'll add a bit of garlic, onion, lemon juice, Parmesan, fresh chives, and plenty of butter crackers for scooping. This one's a showstopper!

1 tablespoon extra virgin olive oil

1 small onion, finely chopped

1 clove garlic, minced

2 (6-ounce) cans lump crabmeat

1 teaspoon Worcestershire sauce

1 tablespoon fresh lemon juice

1 (8-ounce) package cream cheese, at room temperature

½ cup mayonnaise

½ cup plus 2 tablespoons grated Parmesan cheese

2 tablespoons chopped fresh chives

Ground black pepper

2 big sleeves butter crackers (such as Ritz), for serving

1 Preheat the oven to broil, with a rack about 4 inches from the heat.

2 Heat the olive oil in a 10-inch cast iron skillet over medium-high heat. When the oil is shimmering, add the onion and sauté until softened and beginning to brown, about 5 minutes. Add the garlic and crabmeat and stir to combine.

3 Reduce the heat to medium-low. Add the Worcestershire, lemon juice, cream cheese, mayonnaise, ½ cup of the Parmesan, the chives, and a pinch of pepper. Stir to melt and incorporate all of the ingredients. Remove from the heat.

4 Sprinkle the remaining 2 tablespoons Parmesan over the skillet and carefully transfer to the broiler. Broil until the dip is browned and bubbling, about 1 minute.

5 Serve the hot crab dip immediately (being mindful that the pan is scorching hot!), with plenty of butter crackers alongside for scooping.

PEARS & FENNEL

WITH

CRUNCHY CRUMBS

⊰ SERVES 4 TO 6 ⊱

PEARS AND FENNEL ARE LIKE TONY BENNETT and Lady Gaga—the combo may be surprising, but it works. We'll roast the sweet pears and earthy fennel together, just until they begin to yield, then top the lot with an herby bread crumb mixture that crisps and browns beautifully with a bit more time in the oven. I served this as my new Thanksgiving side dish last year, though it's equally welcome on a humbler plate of simple roast chicken or pork tenderloin.

2 medium bulbs fennel, cored and cut into ½-inch-thick wedges

3 Bosc pears, cored and cut into ½-inch-thick wedges

4 tablespoons extra virgin olive oil

Kosher salt

1 cup panko bread crumbs

1 teaspoon chopped fresh thyme leaves

2 teaspoons garlic powder

1 teaspoon herbes de Provence

¼ teaspoon ground black pepper

1 Preheat the oven to 350°F, with a rack in the center position.

2 Toss the fennel and pears in a 9 × 13-inch baking dish with 2 tablespoons of the olive oil and a pinch of salt. Arrange in an even layer and bake until crisp at the edges and tender within, 20 to 30 minutes.

3 Meanwhile, in a small bowl, mix together the panko, thyme, garlic powder, herbes de Provence, the remaining 2 tablespoons olive oil, ½ teaspoon salt, and the pepper.

4 Remove the baking dish from the oven, scatter the panko mixture generously over the hot pears and fennel, and return to the oven to bake until the crumbs are deeply brown and crisp, 25 minutes longer.

5 Allow to cool for 5 to 10 minutes before serving warm.

UNFRIED
MOZZARELLA MARINARA

⊱ **SERVES 6 TO 8** ⊰

IF FRIED MOZZARELLA STICKS WERE A SONG, they'd anchor the sound track to my youth. I remember consistently ordering them, hot and gooey, from the snack bar at the pool or roller rink, and also at a fine culinary establishment in Pennsylvania called Al E. Gators, where pretty much everything on the menu was fried and someone in a giant plush alligator costume would sporadically drop by your table to wave hello with a fuzzy green gator claw. Nowadays, I still enjoy a good mozzarella stick, though I've figured out a way to bake rather than fry them, and thus feel ever so slightly better about my life choices. They're still gooey, still slathered with warm marinara sauce . . . though roller skates and gator costumes are sold separately, I'm told.

These take a bit of planning, since the unbaked cheese sticks need to chill in the freezer before baking, but the good news is that you can assemble and freeze them well in advance—just stick them in a zip-top freezer bag, where they'll last for weeks. Bake them off whenever that craving for warm mozzarella sticks strikes.

¼ cup Italian-style bread crumbs

¼ cup panko bread crumbs

3 tablespoons grated Parmesan cheese

2 teaspoons dried oregano

2 teaspoons garlic powder

½ teaspoon smoked paprika

¼ cup all-purpose flour

Ground black pepper

1 large egg

12 mozzarella string cheeses, halved to make 24 pieces

2 cups store-bought marinara sauce (I like Rao's)

1 Preheat the oven to 400°F, with a rack in the center position.

2 Spread both types of bread crumbs in an even layer on a dry sheet pan. Toast in the oven until deeply golden brown, about 10 minutes. Remove and allow the bread crumbs to cool completely. Turn the oven off.

3 In a medium bowl, mix together the toasted bread crumbs, Parmesan, oregano, garlic powder, and paprika. In another medium bowl, mix the flour with a pinch of pepper. In a small bowl, whisk the egg.

4 Mist the same sheet pan, now empty, with cooking spray or line with parchment paper.

5 Dip each piece of string cheese first in the flour mixture, shaking off any excess, then in the egg, allowing any excess to drip off, and finally in the bread crumb mixture, pressing to coat. Place the coated cheese sticks on the prepared sheet pan, leaving enough space in the middle of the pan for a small ovenproof bowl or ramekin. Freeze the coated cheese sticks for at least 30 minutes, or until you're ready to bake them.

6 Preheat the oven to 400°F. Mist the chilled mozzarella sticks with cooking spray. Nestle a small ovenproof bowl or ramekin filled with marinara sauce onto the pan.

7 Transfer to the oven and bake until the sticks are hot and golden but still hold their shape and the sauce is warm, about 10 minutes. Serve immediately.

PAN CON TOMATE

THIS FANCY-SOUNDING DISH IS ACTUALLY supremely simple—it's just a Spanish-style toast with tomato, garlic, olive oil, and some flaky sea salt for good measure. Since we're dealing with just a few ingredients, you want to make sure you've got the best of the best—the tenderest baguette, the ripest summer tomato, and that good olive oil you've been saving in the back of the cupboard. For this bright, fresh toast, it's definitely worth it. I like to serve these tomato toasts as stand-alone appetizers, or alongside a big summer salad when it's too hot for "real" cooking.

3 large tomatoes

1 baguette, halved horizontally, both halves cut into 6 pieces, each about 4 inches long

1 clove garlic, peeled

¼ cup extra virgin olive oil

Flaky sea salt

1 Preheat the oven to broil, with a rack about 4 inches from the heat.

2 Use the largest holes of a box grater to grate the tomatoes into a large bowl, discarding the skin.

3 Place the baguette slices on a sheet pan, cut-side up. Place under the broiler and broil until charred and toasty, about 1 minute (keep an eye on them—the whole thing happens quickly).

4 Remove and immediately rub the cut sides with the garlic and drizzle with the olive oil. Spoon the grated tomato over the bread and sprinkle liberally with sea salt.

5 Serve warm or at room temperature.

ARTICHOKE GRATIN

◁ SERVES 4 TO 6 ▷

THIS ONE IS QUITE RICH WITH BUTTER, MILK, and cheese (plus some sharp onion and briny artichoke), so it calls for something fresh on top—I like a healthy sprinkle of chopped parsley, and plenty of crisp apple slices for serving. The warm/cool, creamy/crunchy combination is a real treat

2 tablespoons unsalted butter

½ medium shallot, chopped

2 cloves garlic, finely chopped

3 tablespoons all-purpose flour

¼ cup milk

2 (6-ounce) cans marinated artichoke hearts, drained, ½ cup marinade reserved

1 cup shredded Swiss cheese (4 ounces)

½ cup grated Parmesan cheese

2 tablespoons chopped fresh flat-leaf parsley

Apple slices, crackers, or chips, for scooping

1   Preheat the oven to broil, with a rack 4 inches from the heat.

2   Melt the butter in a 10-inch cast iron skillet over medium-high heat. Add the shallot and sauté until translucent, about 4 minutes. Add the garlic and flour, stirring to incorporate, and cook for 1 minute. Whisk in the milk (the mixture will become thick) and reserved artichoke marinade. Add the artichoke hearts and Swiss cheese, and stir to combine.

3   Top the skillet with the Parmesan. Transfer to the broiler and broil until the top is browned and bubbling, 1 to 2 minutes.

4   Scatter the chopped parsley over the skillet. Serve the dip warm, with apple slices, crackers, or chips for scooping.

BROILED WATERMELON WITH BALSAMIC & FETA

≻ SERVES 6 TO 8 ≺

THIS DISH IS FABULOUS FOR SUMMER—SO simple and really stunning. The contrast of warm, balsamic-drizzled watermelon with cool, crisp, lightly dressed greens is hard to beat. Broiling the melon brings out its juicy flavor, so even if you're working with a less-than-stellar crop of fruit, the end result will taste like summer on a plate.

1 baby watermelon (about 8 inches long), rind removed, sliced into 1-inch-thick half-moons (about 3 cups cut)

2 tablespoons balsamic vinegar

2 tablespoons extra virgin olive oil, plus more for the arugula

Kosher salt and ground black pepper

¾ cup crumbled feta cheese

¼ cup chopped fresh mint

5 ounces baby arugula

1　Preheat the oven to broil, with a rack about 4 inches from the heat. Line a sheet pan with foil or mist with cooking spray.

2　Arrange the watermelon slices on the prepared sheet pan and drizzle with the vinegar, olive oil, and a pinch each of kosher salt and pepper. Divide the crumbled feta among the slices (about 1 tablespoon each).

3　In a large bowl, toss together the mint, arugula, ½ teaspoon salt, ¼ teaspoon pepper, and a drizzle of olive oil until the greens are lightly dressed.

4　Broil the watermelon until the feta is well browned, about 3 minutes. Immediately top the watermelon with the dressed greens. Plate and serve the dish right away, while the watermelon is still warm.

ZUCCHINI CAKES
WITH
CRÈME FRAÎCHE

>⊙ **MAKES 12 CAKES** ⊙<

THESE DELICATE LITTLE CAKES ARE PACKED with fresh zucchini, scallions, and a bit of lemon zest, relying on creamy ricotta, some egg, and crisp bread crumbs to hold them together. They're both elegant and punchy, as happy on a fancy platter at cocktail hour as they are served alongside a thick slice of rustic Tomato Galette with Savory Oat Crumble (page 99). Just don't forget the crème fraîche and chopped fresh chives for topping (we're fancy!).

2 medium zucchini, grated on the large holes of a box grater (about 3 cups)

Kosher salt

½ cup whole-milk ricotta cheese

1 large egg

½ cup bread crumbs

3 scallions, white and light green parts only, finely chopped

1 heaping teaspoon grated lemon zest

Ground black pepper

½ cup crème fraîche, for topping

¼ cup chopped fresh chives, for topping

1   Preheat the oven to 350°F, with a rack set in the center position. Grease a 12-cup muffin tin with butter or cooking spray.

2   Place the zucchini in a clean kitchen towel and sprinkle with about ½ teaspoon salt. Gather up the ends of the towel and wring out the zucchini over the sink, squeezing tightly (it should give up a fair bit of liquid).

3   Pat the zucchini dry with paper towels and transfer to a large bowl. Add the ricotta, egg, bread crumbs, scallions, lemon zest, and a pinch of salt and pepper and stir until well combined.

4   Spoon the zucchini mixture evenly into the prepared muffin cups, pressing gently to form little cakes.

5   Transfer the muffin tin to the oven and bake until the cakes are browned and crisp at the edges, 20 to 25 minutes.

6   Allow to cool for about 10 minutes before turning the cakes out of the pan and placing on a serving platter.

7   Top each zucchini cake with a heaping teaspoon of crème fraîche and a sprinkling of chopped chives.

CHEDDAR & HERB
MONKEY BREAD

⊶ SERVES 6 TO 8 ⊷

GOOD NEWS—SAVORY MONKEY BREAD IS totally a thing! Instead of sugar and spice, we're packing this with herbs, garlic, and a respectable amount of cheese. Whether you use store-bought dough or make your own from scratch, consider yourself warned—sharp (cheddar) curves ahead. This bread is addicting. Handle with care.

8 tablespoons (1 stick) unsalted butter, melted and cooled, plus more for greasing the pan

½ teaspoon dried thyme

2 teaspoons chopped fresh flat-leaf parsley

2 teaspoons chopped fresh dill

3 cloves garlic, minced

1 cup shredded cheddar cheese (4 ounces)

2 (8-ounce) cans refrigerated buttermilk biscuit dough, biscuits quartered, or homemade dough (see page 72)

1 Preheat the oven to 350°F, with a rack in the center position. Grease a 12-cup Bundt pan with butter or cooking spray.

2 In a medium bowl, stir together the melted butter, thyme, parsley, dill, and garlic. Place the cheddar in a small bowl.

3 Dunk each piece of dough into the herb butter, then roll in the cheddar. Place the coated dough balls into the prepared Bundt pan, spacing them about ½ inch apart and creating layers.

4 Transfer to the oven and bake until the bread is fragrant and very brown, with a dark, cheesy crust, 25 to 30 minutes.

5 Let the bread cool in the pan for 5 to 10 minutes before carefully inverting onto a large plate or serving platter. Serve warm.

DIY DOUGH!

HERE'S HOW TO MAKE THE DOUGH FROM scratch—you'll need:

2 teaspoons rapid-rise yeast

1⅓ cups barely warm water

2 tablespoons extra virgin olive oil

3½ cups all-purpose flour

2 teaspoons kosher salt

1 In a large bowl (or in a stand mixer fitted with the dough hook), mix the yeast and water and let it sit for 5 minutes. Add the olive oil, flour, and salt and mix to form a dough. With well-floured hands (or the dough hook), knead the dough until cohesive and elastic.

2 Transfer the dough to a large bowl misted with cooking spray. Cover with a clean kitchen towel and allow the dough to sit in a warm corner of the kitchen until doubled in size, about 1 hour.

3 When the dough has doubled in size, flour your hands, punch it down, and break off pieces the size of golf balls, rolling each into a smooth ball. Coat the balls and layer them in the pan, according to the recipe's instructions. Then cover the Bundt with a clean kitchen towel and let the dough rise once more, this time for 15 to 20 minutes, before baking as instructed.

HERBY
TWICE-BAKED
POTATOES

SERVES 4

TWICE-BAKED POTATOES FEEL LIKE A WARM hug from your grandma, you know? They're so full of love (and butter and sour cream and cheese) that they need to be baked not once, but twice. I like to fill mine with lots of punchy fresh herbs to balance out the richness of the dairy, which gives the mounded potatoes a pretty, green-flecked appearance.

If you're short on time, you can bake, scoop, and mix the filling and assemble the potatoes the night before serving; just wrap them tightly and store them in the fridge before giving them their second bake.

4 russet potatoes

1 tablespoon extra virgin olive oil

8 tablespoons (1 stick) unsalted butter, at room temperature

½ cup sour cream

¼ cup grated Parmesan cheese, plus more for sprinkling

2 cloves garlic, finely chopped

¼ cup chopped fresh parsley

¼ cup chopped fresh chives

3 tablespoons chopped fresh tarragon

½ teaspoon kosher salt

½ teaspoon ground black pepper

1 Preheat the oven to 400°F, with a rack in the center position. Line a sheet pan with foil and mist with cooking spray.

2 Rub the potatoes with olive oil and arrange on the sheet pan. Transfer to the oven and bake until fork-tender, about 1 hour. Remove the potatoes from the oven and reduce the oven temperature to 350°F.

3 When the potatoes are cool enough to handle, about 15 minutes, halve them lengthwise and use a spoon to scoop the fleshy centers out into a bowl. Leave the potato skin shells on the pan.

4 Mash the warm potato flesh with the butter, sour cream, Parmesan, garlic, herbs, salt, and pepper until well mixed but still slightly chunky. Mound the mashed potatoes back into the potato shells and sprinkle with a bit of Parmesan.

5 Return the pan to the oven and bake until the stuffed potatoes are hot throughout, 20 to 25 minutes. Serve warm.

MANCHEGO SPINACH PIES

SERVES 8 TO 12

2 (10-ounce) packages frozen spinach, thawed and chopped

6 ounces Manchego cheese, grated (about 2 cups), plus more for sprinkling

3 large eggs

½ cup minced onion

1 tablespoon minced garlic

1 tablespoon chopped fresh dill

1 teaspoon chopped fresh thyme leaves

1 teaspoon grated lemon zest

Pinch of ground nutmeg

2 tablespoons extra virgin olive oil

Kosher salt and ground black pepper

1 sheet frozen puff pastry (from a 17.3-ounce package), thawed (see tip, page 88)

TRADITIONALLY, SPINACH LIKES TO BE PAIRED with feta, but I love the combination of the earthy, sweet green with firm, buttery Manchego cheese. I round out the happy new couple with minced garlic, fresh herbs, lemon zest, and a hint of nutmeg, and then wrap it all up in a cute puff pastry package! The puffy little pies are quite green, slightly nutty, and plenty buttery—a welcome addition to the appetizer rotation, and also very nice served alongside a bowl of Jane's Carrot Potato Soup (page 100).

1 Place the spinach in a clean kitchen towel and squeeze out as much liquid as you can. Transfer to a medium bowl and add the Manchego, eggs, onion, garlic, dill, thyme, lemon zest, nutmeg, olive oil, and a pinch each of salt and pepper.

2 On a well-floured work surface, roll the puff pastry into a 14-inch square. Cut the puff pastry into 4 equal strips, then cut each strip into 3 even rectangles. You will end up with 12 rectangles of dough.

3 Place a rectangle of puff pastry in each cup of a 12-cup muffin tin, arranging the tips so they point up and out. Divide the spinach mixture evenly among the cups, filling each three-fourths full (you may end up with a small bit of leftover filling). Sprinkle some Manchego on top of each cup and fold the pointy edges of the dough over the filling as best you can.

4 Chill the unbaked pies in the refrigerator for 20 minutes, or in the freezer for 10. Meanwhile, preheat the oven to 400°F, with a rack in the center position.

5 Transfer the muffin tin to the oven and bake until the puff pastry is browned all over, 25 to 30 minutes.

6 Serve the pies warm or at room temperature. Leftovers will keep, well wrapped in the refrigerator, for 3 to 4 days. Place on a sheet pan and recrisp in a 350°F oven for about 10 minutes before serving.

PIGS
IN
POLENTA
CAKES

MY FAVORITE THING ABOUT THIS DISH IS that it's just a fancy way to eat hot dogs. Because if we make soft, tender polenta muffins from scratch, and just tuck the hot dogs gently inside before baking, that's considered absolutely sophisticated, right? No need to answer right away. Try one first, maybe! Slightly sweet, plenty savory, and absolutely satisfying, these little cakes give hot dogs (or sausages, which you're welcome to use, too) a good name.

1½ cups all-purpose flour

¾ cup cake flour

1¼ cups polenta

¼ cup sugar

1 tablespoon baking powder

1 teaspoon baking soda

1 teaspoon kosher salt

3 large eggs

1⅓ cups buttermilk

8 tablespoons (1 stick) unsalted butter, at room temperature, plus more for greasing the pan

⅓ cup extra virgin olive oil

¼ cup chopped fresh chives

4 hot dogs or fully cooked sausages, halved lengthwise, then cut crosswise into thirds (24 pieces total)

1 Preheat the oven to 375°F, with a rack in the center position. Grease a 12-cup muffin tin with butter or cooking spray.

2 In a medium bowl, mix together the flours, polenta, sugar, baking powder, baking soda, and salt. In a separate medium bowl, whisk together the eggs and buttermilk until well combined.

3 In a stand mixer fitted with the paddle attachment, beat together the butter and olive oil until combined. Add the flour mixture and slowly beat until coarse crumbs form. Add the egg-buttermilk mixture and continue mixing just until the batter comes together. Fold in the chives.

4 Evenly distribute the batter among the muffin cups, filling each almost to the rim. Press 2 pieces of hot dog or sausage into the middle of each.

5 Transfer to the oven and bake until a tester inserted into the center of the largest muffin comes out clean, 20 to 25 minutes.

6 Allow to cool for about 10 minutes before turning the cakes out onto a serving platter. Serve warm or at room temperature.

APPLE SLICE
TUNA
MELTS

⊱ **MAKES 8 PIECES** ⊰

AFTER YEARS OF PUTTING CHOPPED APPLE in my tuna salad (the crunch! the sweetness! so good), I wondered if I shouldn't mix things up a bit. This new tuna salad is gently spiced with Dijon and curry powder, served *over* thinly sliced apples. Topped with cheddar and gently warmed in the oven, the result is a fun twist on the traditional tuna melt, small and pretty enough to serve at the appetizer table, yet substantial enough to serve as an accompaniment to a big salad or bowl of soup as a main course.

2 large apples (I like Honeycrisp)

1 (12.8-ounce) can water-packed chunk light tuna, drained

3 scallions, white and light green parts only, finely chopped, plus more for garnish

¼ cup capers, drained

¼ cup raisins

¼ cup mayonnaise

1½ tablespoons Dijon mustard

1 tablespoon curry powder

Kosher salt and ground black pepper

8 slices sharp cheddar cheese

1 Preheat the oven to 375°F, with a rack in the center position. Line a sheet pan with foil or parchment paper.

2 Slice the apples vertically into ½-inch-thick, round slices, discarding the rounded end pieces (chef's snack!) and trimming the core slice of seeds and stem. Place the apple rounds on the prepared sheet pan, spacing them evenly apart.

3 In a medium bowl, mix together the tuna, scallions, capers, raisins, mayonnaise, mustard, curry powder, and a pinch each of salt and pepper. Mound the tuna salad evenly on the apple slices and place a slice of cheddar over each.

4 Transfer to the oven and bake until the tuna salad is warmed through, the cheese is melted, and the apple slices are warm but still crisp, about 10 minutes.

5 Top each open-faced sandwich with an extra sprinkle of chopped scallions and serve warm.

CHAPTER THREE

VEGGIE
MAINS

Truffle Mushroom Lasagna 94

Pesto Zoodle Casserole 96

Baked Tortellini with White Beans,
Kale & Tomato Sauce 103

Baked Spring Risotto 83

Portobello & Black Bean Chili 90

Moroccan Tomato Soup with
Chickpeas ➕ 93

Jane's Carrot Potato Soup ➕ 100

Curried Red Lentil Soup 102

Broccoli Parmesan Soup ➕ 105

Linguine Primavera 109

Ultimate Oven Mac & Cheese ➕ 110

Red Curry Squash Bowls with Chickpeas 84

Baked Eggplant Parmesan 87

Greens & Goat Tart 88

Charred Sichuan Green Beans & Tofu 91

Tomato Galette with Savory Oat Crumble 99

Crispy Tomato & Butter Bean Skillet 80

Brown Butter Squash Agnolotti 97

Wilted Arugula & Sweet Pea Cheese
Ravioli 106

CRISPY TOMATO & BUTTER BEAN SKILLET

SERVES 4

THIS HEARTY, COMFORTING DISH WAS INSPIRED by one of my favorite dishes at a restaurant called Westward in Seattle. The rich, sweet smell that wafted from the bubbling skillet the first time I ordered it, full of saucy, tomato-laden beans, salty cheese, and crisp bread crumbs, had me swooning in my chair and vowing to re-create the dish at home. The restaurant's version uses gigante beans and fresh marjoram, but I like using canned butter beans and fresh rosemary, which are easier to find in most grocery stores. Just be sure to serve the skillet with plenty of crusty bread for dipping.

¼ cup plus 1 tablespoon extra virgin olive oil

1 medium yellow onion, finely chopped (about 1½ cups)

4 cloves garlic, finely chopped (about 4 teaspoons)

2 teaspoons finely chopped fresh rosemary

2 cups store-bought marinara sauce (I like Rao's)

3 (15-ounce) cans butter beans, drained and rinsed

2 ounces crumbled feta cheese (about ½ cup)

1¼ cups panko bread crumbs

2 teaspoons chopped fresh thyme leaves

1 teaspoon kosher salt

½ teaspoon ground black pepper

1   Preheat the oven to 350°F, with a rack in the center position.

2   Heat 1 tablespoon of the olive oil in a 10-inch cast iron skillet over medium-high heat. When the oil is shimmering, add the onion and cook until just starting to brown, 5 to 7 minutes. Stir in the garlic and rosemary and sauté for another minute. Add the marinara sauce, beans, and feta, stirring to combine. Reduce the heat to low.

3   While the beans are heating on the stove, in a small bowl, mix together the panko, thyme, remaining ¼ cup olive oil, salt, and pepper.

4   Generously sprinkle the bread crumb mixture over the skillet of beans. Transfer to the oven and bake until the beans are bubbling and the topping is browned and crisp, 20 to 30 minutes.

5   Serve hot, with lots of bread for sopping up the sauce.

BAKED SPRING RISOTTO

⟨ SERVES 4 TO 6 ⟩

2 tablespoons extra virgin olive oil

1 cup chopped shallots (about 2 medium)

1 tablespoon garlic powder

1½ cups Arborio rice

Kosher salt and ground black pepper

4 cups vegetable broth

1 cup frozen peas

12 ounces frozen artichoke hearts (about 2 cups)

12 ounces frozen asparagus tips, spears, or cuts (about 2 cups)

2 cups grated Parmesan cheese (about 8 ounces)

4 ounces mascarpone cheese

¼ cup chopped fresh chives

½ cup chopped or chiffonade-cut fresh basil (see tip below)

I LOVE THE CREAMY, STARCHY, SPECIAL-occasion-ness of risotto, but standing over the stove, stirring constantly to ensure the perfect consistency? No thanks. This one-pot, mostly hands-off version, full of spring flavor, is definitely where it's at. And the best part? We can have this verdant, springy treat any time of year, since the recipe relies on using frozen artichoke hearts, asparagus pieces, and peas, which seem to work better than the fresh stuff, both texture- and flavor-wise.

1   Preheat the oven to 375°F, with a rack in the center position.

2   Heat the olive oil in a 5- to 6-quart Dutch oven over medium-high heat. When the oil is shimmering, add the shallots and sauté until soft, about 5 minutes. Add the garlic powder, rice, and a pinch each of salt and pepper, stirring to coat. Toast the rice for about 2 minutes, then add the broth and bring to a boil.

3   Cover the pot and place it in the oven. Bake until the rice is almost tender, 30 to 40 minutes. Add the frozen vegetables and 1 cup of the Parmesan, cover the pot, and continue baking for 10 to 15 minutes longer to heat everything through.

4   Remove the pot from the oven and stir in the mascarpone cheese. Serve the risotto hot, with the remaining Parmesan, chives, and basil scattered on top.

HOW TO? DO THE CHIFFONADE

The word *chiffonade* may sound fancy (it comes from French, after all), but it just means to slice leafy herbs like basil or mint into fine, delicate shreds. To do it, simply stack your leaves on top of one another, roll them up lengthwise into a tight little cigar, then slice the cigar crosswise into thin strips. Fluff up the strips with your fingers—you've just made a chiffonade!

RED CURRY SQUASH BOWLS WITH CHICKPEAS

> SERVES 4

SWEET, ROASTED SQUASH FILLED WITH warmly spiced chickpeas feels like one of the heartiest (and healthiest!) vegetarian options around. Aside from the red curry paste, which you may need to seek out in the Asian foods section of your local supermarket, we make good use of common pantry ingredients here. And if you have the foresight to roast the squash ahead of time (the day before serving, say), the whole thing comes together in a snap.

2 small butternut squash, halved lengthwise and seeded

4 tablespoons extra virgin olive oil

Kosher salt

2 tablespoons Thai red curry paste

1 (13.5-ounce) can coconut milk

1 (15-ounce) can chickpeas, drained and rinsed

1 small red bell pepper, chopped

4 scallions, white and light green parts only, chopped

¼ cup chopped fresh cilantro

1 Preheat the oven to 400°F, with a rack in the center position. Line a sheet pan with foil and mist with cooking spray.

2 Place the squash halves on the prepared sheet pan, brush each with 1 tablespoon of the olive oil, and sprinkle each with a pinch of salt. Turn the squash cut-side down, transfer to the oven, and roast until the skins are beginning to brown and wrinkle, and the flesh is fork-tender, about 40 minutes. Remove from the oven and set aside to cool slightly. (Leave the oven on.)

3 While the squash cooks, place the curry paste in a medium bowl and slowly whisk in the coconut milk until smooth. Add the chickpeas, bell pepper, and scallions and stir to combine.

4 When the squash halves are cool enough to handle, flip them over and scoop out most of the flesh to form "bowls." Combine the scooped-out flesh with the chickpeas and fill the squash bowls with the chickpea mixture, mounding each one high. Return the pan to the oven and bake until warmed through, about 15 minutes.

5 Top the curry squash bowls with the cilantro and serve warm.

HOW TO? WORK WITH COCONUT MILK

Before opening a can of coconut milk, be sure to shake it vigorously. This helps homogenize the milk, which often separates (the thick cream rising to the top, the thinner water collecting at the bottom) when the can is left to sit on the shelf.

BAKED EGGPLANT PARMESAN

SERVES 4

THIS RECIPE OFFERS A LIGHTENED-UP VERSION of an Italian-American classic. Roasting the eggplant gives it a sweetness and creaminess that just can't be beat. And topping it with crispy, spiced bread crumbs, simple tomato sauce, and plenty of cheese? Winner winner, eggplant dinner!

2 large eggs

1½ cups panko bread crumbs

2 teaspoons garlic powder

2 teaspoons dried oregano

2 tablespoons sweet or smoked paprika

1 teaspoon kosher salt

2 tablespoons extra virgin olive oil

1½ medium eggplants, sliced into ½-inch-thick rounds (about 16 slices)

1 (24-ounce) jar store-bought marinara sauce (I like Rao's)

½ pound sliced provolone cheese (about 12 slices)

¼ cup grated Parmesan cheese

1 Preheat the oven to 375°F, with a rack in the center position. Line a sheet pan with foil and mist with cooking spray.

2 In a medium bowl, whisk the eggs until smooth. In another medium bowl, stir together the panko, garlic powder, oregano, paprika, salt, and olive oil until combined.

3 Dip each slice of eggplant first into the beaten egg, allowing the excess to drip off, and then into the panko mixture, pressing to coat. Place the coated eggplant slices on the prepared sheet pan, nestling them as close together as possible. Mist the eggplant with cooking spray.

4 Transfer to the oven and bake for 30 minutes.

5 Remove from the oven, carefully flip each slice of eggplant, and evenly distribute the marinara sauce over the slices. Top with the provolone cheese and Parmesan. Return to the oven and bake until the eggplant is tender and the cheese is melted and bubbling, 10 to 15 minutes.

6 Serve the eggplant parm hot.

GREENS & GOAT TART

> ⌐ SERVES 6 TO 8 ⌐

THIS IS THE WAY TO GET YOUR GREENS! PILED on top of buttery pastry dough and flecked with herby goat cheese and chopped pistachios. The combination of crisp crust, creamy cheese, lightly charred greens, and crunchy nuts is a hard one to beat. If you're (like, totally) over kale, feel free to vary up the leafy greens and use collards, mustard greens, Swiss chard, or the like. This tart does well as an appetizer, cut into smaller, daintier squares, but I like to serve it in fat rectangles as a main course, with a green salad or some roasted tomatoes alongside.

HOW TO?
THAW PUFF PASTRY

To thaw puff pastry, simply place the box in the refrigerator overnight! Or take a sheet of dough out of the box (keeping it in its parchment wrapping) and set it on the counter at room temperature for about 30 minutes, until it's pliable but still quite cold—you should be able to unfold the sheet of dough without it cracking.

1 sheet frozen puff pastry (from a 17.3-ounce package), thawed (see tip below)

12 ounces herbed goat cheese

2 cloves garlic, minced

4 scallions, white and light green parts only, finely chopped

1 small bunch lacinato kale, stemmed and roughly chopped

2 tablespoons extra virgin olive oil

Kosher salt and ground black pepper

¼ cup chopped pistachios

¼ cup chopped fresh flat-leaf parsley

1 Preheat the oven to 400°F, with a rack in the center position. Line a sheet pan with parchment paper.

2 On a lightly floured surface, roll the puff pastry out into a 12 × 17-inch rectangle. Carefully transfer the pastry to the prepared pan and place the pan in the refrigerator to chill, about 20 minutes.

3 Spread 8 ounces of the goat cheese thinly over the chilled puff pastry (or if it's too difficult to spread, break it into little pieces and scatter them evenly over the dough), leaving a 1-inch border around the edges. Sprinkle the garlic and scallions over the goat cheese.

4 Spread the kale over the garlic and scallions, leaving the bare border intact. Drizzle with the olive oil and sprinkle with a big pinch each of salt and pepper. Massage the kale with your fingers to distribute the olive oil and seasonings evenly, then crumble the remaining goat cheese over the layer of kale and top with the pistachios.

5 Transfer to the oven and bake until the crust is deep brown and the greens are wilted and charred at the edges, about 30 minutes.

6 Sprinkle parsley over the warm tart and allow to cool slightly before slicing into squares. Serve warm or at room temperature.

PORTOBELLO
& BLACK BEAN
CHILI

⊰ SERVES 6 TO 8 ⊱

IN MOST PLACES, CHILI RECIPES ARE ALL about the meat (in Texas especially, so I'm told)—but why should carnivores get all of that hearty, spicy, chili love? Using finely chopped portobello mushrooms mimics the heft and texture of meat, while giving this strictly veggie chili amazing depth of flavor. Plenty of spice, smoky chipotle flavor, and black beans round out this nourishing bowl of comfort.

5 tablespoons extra virgin olive oil

2 small yellow onions, chopped (about 3 cups)

5 portobello mushrooms, finely chopped

3 cloves garlic, minced

2 tablespoons chili powder

2 teaspoons ground cumin

2 teaspoons sweet or smoked paprika

1 teaspoon kosher salt

2 tablespoons tomato paste

2 red bell peppers, chopped

2 chipotles in adobo sauce, chopped

1 (28-ounce) can diced tomatoes plus 1 (15-ounce) can diced tomatoes

3 (15-ounce) cans black beans, drained and rinsed

2 cups vegetable broth

Chili fixings, like chopped scallions, sour cream, and chips

1 Preheat the oven to 450°F, with a rack in the center position.

2 Heat 2 tablespoons of the olive oil in a medium (5- to 6-quart) Dutch oven over medium-high heat. When the oil is shimmering, add the onions and sauté until soft, 5 to 10 minutes. Add the mushrooms and remaining 3 tablespoons olive oil, stirring to coat. Stir in the garlic, chili powder, cumin, paprika, and salt and cook for 1 minute.

3 Add the tomato paste, bell peppers, and chipotles and cook until the peppers start to soften, 5 to 7 minutes. Stir in the diced tomatoes, beans, and broth and bring the chili to a simmer.

4 Transfer the pot, uncovered, to the oven and bake until the vegetables are quite tender and the liquid has reduced by an inch or so, about 30 minutes.

5 Serve the chili hot, topped with your favorite fixings.

CHARRED
SICHUAN
GREEN BEANS
& TOFU

SERVES 4

I LOVE ORDERING THE GARLICKY CHARRED green beans at our local Chinese restaurant, so it was only a matter of time before I got the itch to re-create the dish at home. As it turns out, a few fun spices, a sheet pan, and the broiler are all it takes! Firm tofu, which soaks up the spicy, salty sauce, is a natural pairing.

You can find Sichuan peppercorns and sambal oelek (a spicy, Southeast Asian chile sauce) in the Asian foods section at most well-stocked grocery stores.

HOW TO?
DRAIN TOFU

Ever had bland, soggy tofu? Yuck. Pressing tofu helps dry it out, which improves its texture and flavor. Wrap the block of tofu with paper towels, then place it on a plate or a cutting board. Put a heavy plate or cutting board on top of the tofu and leave it to drain for at least 15 minutes or until you're ready to make dinner.

2 pounds green beans, ends trimmed

2 tablespoons plus 2 teaspoons canola oil

Kosher salt

1 teaspoon Sichuan peppercorns, crushed

1 tablespoon sambal oelek

2 cloves garlic, minced

1 tablespoon minced fresh ginger

2 tablespoons capers, drained

1 tablespoon sugar

3 tablespoons less-sodium soy sauce

2 teaspoons toasted sesame oil

1 (12- to 14-ounce) package firm tofu, drained (see tip below)

¼ cup chopped scallions, white and light green parts only

1 Preheat the oven to broil, with a rack about 4 inches from the heat. Line a sheet pan with foil or mist it with cooking spray.

2 Toss the green beans with 2 tablespoons of the canola oil and a pinch of salt on the prepared sheet pan and spread them out in an even layer.

3 In a small bowl, mix together the remaining 2 teaspoons canola oil, the Sichuan peppercorns, sambal oelek, garlic, ginger, capers, sugar, soy sauce, and sesame oil until smooth. Drizzle half of the sauce over the green beans.

4 Remove the heavy weight and paper towels from the block of tofu, then use a sharp knife to cut the block into 8 rectangles, between ½ and ¾ inch wide. Dredge each piece of tofu in the remaining sauce, then tuck the tofu pieces on top of and around the green beans on the pan. Scatter the scallions on top of the dish.

5 Transfer to the oven and broil until the beans are good and charred, 4 to 6 minutes, flipping the tofu halfway through cooking.

6 Serve hot.

MOROCCAN
TOMATO
SOUP
WITH
CHICKPEAS

⊶ SERVES 4 TO 6 ⊷

HERE'S A FUN TWIST ON CLASSIC TOMATO soup. We still get creaminess, thanks to butter and heaps of chickpeas, but the Moroccan spices (cumin, cinnamon, ginger, and paprika!) add a warm and layered depth of flavor to this rich and satisfying bowl. A generous drizzle of honey at the finish cuts through the sharp acidity of canned tomatoes, so don't skimp.

4 tablespoons unsalted butter

1 yellow onion, chopped

2 large carrots, peeled and chopped

4 stalks celery, chopped

Kosher salt and ground black pepper

4 cloves garlic, finely chopped

2 teaspoons sweet or smoked paprika

½ teaspoon ground cinnamon

½ teaspoon ground cumin

½ teaspoon ground ginger

1 (28-ounce) can whole, peeled tomatoes

2 cups low-sodium vegetable or chicken broth

1 (15-ounce) can chickpeas, drained and rinsed

¼ cup fresh lemon juice

1 heaping tablespoon honey

¼ cup chopped fresh cilantro, for garnish

1 Melt the butter in a medium (5- to 6-quart) Dutch oven over medium-high heat. Add the onion, carrots, celery, and a pinch each of salt and pepper and sauté until the vegetables are tender, about 10 minutes.

2 Add the garlic, paprika, cinnamon, cumin, and ginger, stirring well to combine. Cook 1 minute more. Stir in the tomatoes (and their juices) and the broth.

3 Using an immersion blender (or in a food processor, working in batches), blend the soup until smooth. Return the soup to the pot and cook over medium heat until warmed through. Add the chickpeas, lemon juice, and honey and season with salt and pepper.

4 Serve the soup hot, garnished with a generous sprinkling of cilantro.

TRUFFLE MUSHROOM LASAGNA

⌐ SERVES 6 TO 8 ⌐

EVEN AS A LIFELONG, CARD-CARRYING Meat Eater, this is my favorite lasagna recipe, full stop. Earthy mushrooms are the perfect complement to the creamy ricotta and mozzarella cheeses; and a nice hit of truffle oil takes the whole thing from ho-hum to hummina hummina. Using no-boil noodles (and blitzing the mushrooms in the food processor, if you'd like) helps speed up the assembly of the lasagna, which can either be baked straightaway, or covered tightly and frozen until the warm, cheesy, truffled craving strikes. For the ricotta and the mozzarella, either part skim or whole milk will work.

SUBBING OUT

If you don't want to invest in a jar of truffle oil, use any fresh, flavorful extra virgin olive oil instead. The resulting lasagna won't be "truffled," but it'll be delicious nonetheless.

15 ounces ricotta cheese

½ cup grated Parmesan cheese, plus more for topping

¼ cup shredded low-moisture mozzarella cheese, plus more for topping

1 teaspoon dried oregano

1 teaspoon garlic powder

1 large egg

3 tablespoons white truffle oil

Kosher salt and ground black pepper

1 pound cremini mushrooms (about 2 cups), finely chopped

2 cups store-bought marinara sauce (I like Rao's)

8 ounces no-boil lasagna noodles (about 15 noodles)

1 Preheat the oven to 375°F, with a rack in the center position.

2 In a medium bowl, mix together the ricotta, Parmesan, mozzarella, oregano, garlic powder, egg, 1 tablespoon of the truffle oil, and a pinch each of salt and pepper.

3 In a medium bowl, mix together the chopped mushrooms and remaining 2 tablespoons truffle oil.

4 Spread ½ cup of the marinara sauce into the bottom of a 9 × 13-inch baking dish. Top with a layer of tightly packed noodles. Spread one-third of the ricotta mixture over the noodles, then top with half of the mushroom mixture. Spread another ½ cup of the sauce over the mushrooms, top with more noodles, another one-third of the ricotta mixture, and the rest of the mushrooms. For the last layer, start with ½ cup marinara, then noodles, then the remaining ricotta mixture, and finally the remaining ½ cup sauce. Top it all with a handful of extra Parmesan and shredded mozzarella.

5 Cover the dish with foil, transfer to the oven, and bake until hot and bubbling, 35 to 45 minutes. Allow to cool slightly before slicing into large squares and serving warm.

PESTO
ZOODLE
CASSEROLE

⊰ SERVES 4 TO 6 ⊱

I WAS SKEPTICAL OF THE WHOLE "ZOODLE" phenomenon at first, but I have to say that making noodles out of zucchini is not only fun but also straight-up delicious. Whether you're avoiding grains or just want to switch things up a bit in the kitchen, zucchini noodles are the perfect anchor for a mess of bright pesto and myriad forms of cheese. As an avid pasta enthusiast, I can happily report that you won't even miss the grains here! Pinky promise.

9 medium zucchini, spiralized (about 10 cups)

1 tablespoon kosher salt

6 ounces pesto

1 cup mozzarella bocconcini, halved

1 cup whole-milk ricotta cheese

¼ cup grated Parmesan cheese

1   Preheat the oven to 350°F, with a rack in the center position. Grease a 9 × 13-inch baking dish with butter or cooking spray.

2   Gather the zoodles together in a clean kitchen towel, sprinkle with the salt, and gently wring to release any extra moisture (you may need to do this in two batches). Place the zoodles in the prepared dish and toss gently with the pesto. Spread the zoodles out evenly over the pan.

3   Tuck the halved bocconcini into and around the zoodles, and dollop the ricotta by the tablespoon over the top. Finish by scattering the Parmesan on top of it all.

4   Transfer to the oven and bake until bubbling and beginning to brown, about 30 minutes.

5   Serve the zoodle casserole warm.

FUN HACK!
ZOODLES OR BUST

If you don't have a spiralizer, don't fret! You can still make beautiful zucchini "noodles" (or carrot noodles, depending on the recipe) using a simple vegetable peeler. Find nice, fat zukes and use long strokes to shave thin, noodly strips from both sides of the vegetable (discard the seedy core). You'll be in (veggie noodle) business in no time.

BROWN BUTTER
SQUASH AGNOLOTTI

SERVES 4

DOCTORING UP STORE-BOUGHT FRESH PASTA dough with brown butter, fresh sage, and roasted squash is a fun and simple way to get an elegant and flavorful meal on the table. So easy! So deliciously autumnal! And all in one pan, of course. If you can't find agnolotti, substitute the same size package of cheese or mushroom ravioli.

4 tablespoons unsalted butter

3 cups peeled and cubed butternut squash

1 teaspoon chopped fresh sage

½ teaspoon kosher salt

¼ teaspoon ground black pepper

2 (9-ounce) packages fresh agnolotti (see tip, page 103)

1 cup vegetable broth

2 tablespoons extra virgin olive oil

½ cup grated Parmesan cheese

1 Preheat the oven to 400°F, with a rack in the center position.

2 Melt the butter in a 10 inch cast iron skillet over medium-high heat. Let the butter bubble, swirling the pan occasionally, until it starts to brown. Remove from the heat.

3 Add the squash, sage, salt, and pepper to the pan and toss to coat in the brown butter. Transfer the pan to the oven and roast until the squash is almost tender, about 20 minutes.

4 Remove from the oven and add the agnolotti, broth, and olive oil to the pan and stir to combine. Cover the pan, return it to the oven, and bake until the pasta is tender, about 10 minutes.

5 Remove the pan from the oven and sprinkle the Parmesan over the pasta. Return the pan to the oven, uncovered, and bake until the cheese is melted, about 5 minutes.

6 Serve hot.

TOMATO GALETTE
WITH
SAVORY OAT CRUMBLE

SERVES 6 TO 8

I LOVE A GOOD GALETTE. A GA-WHAT, YOU SAY? A galette! . . . Basically just a fancy way of saying "free-form pie." Somehow it's both rustic and sophisticated all at once, and this pretty, imperfect sort of pie seems to be the perfect way to showcase a bumper crop of tomatoes (or summer squash, eggplant, potatoes, peppers—the list is endless, it seems). Using store-bought puff pastry makes this oat-and-herb-topped, open-faced pie as easy as, well . . . pie.

1 sheet frozen puff pastry (from a 17.3-ounce package), thawed (see tip, page 88)

¼ cup plus 2 tablespoons old-fashioned rolled oats

¼ cup all-purpose flour

½ teaspoon herbes de Provence

¼ cup grated Parmesan cheese

½ teaspoon kosher salt

¼ teaspoon ground black pepper

3 tablespoons cold unsalted butter, cut into small cubes

½ cup mascarpone cheese

4 medium tomatoes, cut into ¼- to ½-inch-thick slices

1   Preheat the oven to 400°F, with a rack in the center position. Line a sheet pan with parchment paper.

2   On a lightly floured surface, roll the puff pastry out into a 12 × 17-inch rectangle. Carefully transfer the pastry to the prepared pan and place the pan in the refrigerator to chill while you prep the rest of the dish.

3   In a medium bowl, mix together the oats, flour, herbes de Provence, Parmesan, salt, and pepper until combined. Add the butter and work it in with your fingers until crumbly (it should clump together when you squeeze it gently).

4   Spread the mascarpone thinly over the chilled puff pastry, leaving 1 inch bare around the edges. Layer the tomatoes on top of the mascarpone, top with the oat crumble, and fold the edges of the puff pastry up and over the sides to form a rough crust.

5   Transfer to the oven and bake until the crust is deep brown and the filling is bubbling, about 30 minutes.

6   Allow the galette to cool slightly before slicing into squares. Serve warm or at room temperature.

JANE'S CARROT POTATO SOUP

> SERVES 4 TO 6

MY FRIEND JANE MAKES THE BEST SOUP IN the world. When I first tasted this luscious, smooth, gorgeously orange soup, I was hit by such a strong wave of comfort and delight that I sighed audibly and immediately slurped up my entire bowl. How could a simple bowl of soup taste so perfect, so right, so . . . magical? I had to know. Jane explained that the magic is in the simplicity—all it takes are onions, carrots, potatoes, and a healthy amount of butter. I still don't really get it, because on their own, they're just normal, everyday ingredients. But together? Some kind of magic, I'm telling you.

6 tablespoons unsalted butter

1 large yellow onion, roughly chopped

Kosher salt and ground black pepper

3 large russet potatoes, peeled and cut into ¾-inch cubes

1 pound carrots, peeled and chopped

4 cups low-sodium vegetable or chicken broth

½ cup milk or half-and-half

Crusty bread, for serving

1   Melt the butter in a medium (5- to 6-quart) Dutch oven over medium-high heat. Add the onion and a pinch each of salt and pepper and sauté until softened, about 5 minutes.

2   Add the potatoes, carrots, and broth. Bring to a boil, then reduce the heat to low and simmer the soup, covered, until the vegetables are softened, about 20 minutes.

3   Using an immersion blender (or in a food processor, working in batches), blend the soup until smooth. Stir in the milk and season with salt and pepper.

4   Serve the soup hot, with the crusty bread alongside for dipping.

CURRIED RED LENTIL SOUP

> SERVES 4 TO 6

THIS IS THE KIND OF SOUP I FIND THERAPEUTIC—I get happily lost in the chopping, the scent of the warm spices, the stirring and simmering away, and at the end? I can enjoy a steamy bowlful of cozy. It's even better when it has time to sit in the refrigerator, the flavors melding and marrying; so feel free to make it ahead of time and store it in an airtight container, in the fridge (or freezer).

2 tablespoons extra virgin olive oil

1 large yellow onion, finely chopped

3 medium carrots, peeled and chopped

4 stalks celery, chopped

Kosher salt and ground black pepper

2 tablespoons curry powder

¼ teaspoon crushed red pepper

¼ teaspoon ground turmeric

4 cloves garlic, minced

2 cups red lentils

10 cups vegetable broth

1 bay leaf

¼ cup fresh lemon juice

2 cups baby arugula or spinach

Crème fraîche or sour cream, for serving

Chopped fresh chives or cilantro, for serving

1 Heat the olive oil in a medium (5- to 6-quart) or large (7- to 8-quart) Dutch oven over medium-high heat. When the oil is shimmering, add the onion, carrots, celery, 1 teaspoon salt, and a pinch of black pepper and sauté until the vegetables are tender, about 10 minutes. Add the curry powder, crushed red pepper, turmeric, and garlic and cook for 1 minute longer. Stir in the lentils, broth, and bay leaf and bring to a boil. Reduce the heat to low and simmer until the lentils are tender, 20 to 25 minutes.

2 Stir in the lemon juice and greens and taste to adjust the seasonings. Discard the bay leaf.

3 Serve the soup hot, topped with dollops of crème fraîche or sour cream and a sprinkling of fresh herbs.

BAKED TORTELLINI
WITH
WHITE BEANS, KALE & TOMATO SAUCE

SERVES 6 TO 8

ALL HAIL THE PASTA BAKE! SURE, WE COULD dismiss it as old-fashioned and uncool, but then we'd be eating our words as we spooned second helpings of cheesy pasta, tomatoey beans, toothsome kale, and crisp panko topping onto our plates. Yep, there's a reason the pasta bake is the backbone of American home cooking (namely, ease and flavor), so let's not mess with tried-and-true dinnertime success, 'kay?

1 bunch lacinato kale, stemmed and roughly chopped

4 tablespoons extra virgin olive oil

½ teaspoon kosher salt

¼ teaspoon ground black pepper

1 (15-ounce) can cannellini beans, drained and rinsed

2 (9-ounce) packages fresh cheese or spinach tortellini (see tip below)

1 (24-ounce) jar store-bought marinara sauce (I like Rao's)

1 cup vegetable broth

1 cup panko bread crumbs

1 cup shredded Parmesan cheese (4 ounces)

1 teaspoon dried oregano

1   Preheat the oven to 375°F, with a rack in the center position. Mist a 9 × 13-inch baking dish with cooking spray.

2   Toss the kale in the prepared dish with 2 tablespoons of the olive oil, the salt, and pepper until well coated, then mix in the beans and tortellini. Arrange the mixture evenly in the bottom of the pan. Add the sauce and broth, distributing evenly around the pan.

3   Cover with foil, transfer to the oven, and bake until the tortellini are just tender, about 20 minutes.

4   While the pasta bakes, in a small bowl, mix together the panko, Parmesan, oregano, and remaining 2 tablespoons olive oil.

5   When the pasta is just tender, remove the dish from the oven and top the casserole with the panko mixture. Return to the oven and bake until the crumb topping is crisp and browned, about 10 minutes.

6   Serve the casserole hot from the oven.

HOW TO? FIND FRESH PASTA

I love using fresh, stuffed pasta for its great flavor and lightning-fast cook time (just 3 minutes!). You can find it in the refrigerated section of most grocery stores. Tortellini and ravioli are standard, though I've seen more exotic types, like agnolotti, sold in more well-stocked markets.

BROCCOLI PARMESAN SOUP

4 tablespoons unsalted butter

1 medium onion, chopped (about 2 cups)

2 cloves garlic, minced

3 stalks celery, chopped (about 1 cup)

1 large carrot, chopped (about 1½ cups)

1 teaspoon kosher salt

½ teaspoon ground black pepper

½ cup all-purpose flour

1½ cups half-and-half

6 cups low-sodium chicken broth

1 bay leaf

2 pounds broccoli, chopped (or 6 cups chopped broccoli florets and stems)

10 ounces Parmesan cheese, grated (about 2½ cups), plus more for garnish

REMEMBER THAT KIND OF BLAND, KIND OF heavy, orange-and-green-flecked broccoli cheddar soup that was always on offer in the school cafeteria? Well, this broccoli Parmesan soup is like the beautifully mysterious, foreign-exchange-student cousin of broccoli cheddar in the lunch line—it's more sophisticated, better dressed, more richly accented, and, if we're really talking about soup, more delicious than its cousin counterpart. Sure, it'll probably steal your heart spring of junior year three weeks before leaving and vow passionately to keep in touch but then only send you one lousy letter. But even then? It'll be worth it. For the soup, I mean.

1 Melt the butter in a large (7- to 8-quart) Dutch oven over medium-high heat. Add the onion, garlic, celery, carrot, salt, and pepper and cook until the vegetables are just tender, about 7 minutes.

2 Add the flour, stirring thoroughly to incorporate, and cook for 2 minutes. Slowly add the half-and-half, stirring well to prevent lumps from forming. Add the broth, bay leaf, and broccoli.

3 Bring the soup to a boil, then reduce the heat to low and simmer, covered, until the broccoli is very tender, 20 to 30 minutes. Discard the bay leaf.

4 Using an immersion blender (or in a food processor, working in batches), blend the soup until smooth. Slowly whisk in the Parmesan until well incorporated.

5 Taste the soup and adjust the seasonings, if necessary. Serve hot, garnished with a sprinkling of Parmesan.

WILTED ARUGULA

& SWEET PEA

CHEESE RAVIOLI

SERVES 4

THIS DISH IS A FAR CRY FROM THE OVERCOOKED frozen cheese ravioli smothered in red sauce I used to eat as a kid; but even dressed up with wilted greens, sweet peas, and shredded Parmesan, it comes together just as quickly. Fresh ravioli makes a bright, sophisticated meal with "dinner hack" written all over it—and I mean that in the best way possible.

1 tablespoon unsalted butter

1 tablespoon extra virgin olive oil

6 cups baby arugula

½ teaspoon kosher salt

¼ teaspoon ground black pepper

2 (9-ounce) packages fresh cheese ravioli (see tip, page 103)

1 cup frozen peas

1 cup vegetable broth

½ cup shredded Parmesan cheese

2 tablespoons chopped fresh chives

1 Preheat the oven to 400°F, with a rack in the center position.

2 Melt the butter in the olive oil in a 10-inch cast iron skillet over medium-high heat. Add the arugula, a handful or two at a time, adding more as it wilts and stirring to coat. Sprinkle on the salt and pepper.

3 Add the pasta, peas, and broth to the pan and stir to combine. Cover the pan, slide it into the oven, and bake until the pasta is tender, about 10 minutes.

4 Remove the pan from the oven and sprinkle the Parmesan over the pasta. Return the pan to the oven, uncovered, and bake until the cheese is melted, about 5 minutes.

5 Serve hot, sprinkled with the chives.

LINGUINE
PRIMAVERA

⚬ **SERVES 4** ⚬

THIS RECIPE IS JUST PLAIN COOL. WE TAKE dried pasta and cook it in a big pot in the oven with lots of vegetables and a bit of stock, and instead of getting all fussy and clumped, as dried pasta sometimes likes to do, it pulls itself together and *self-sauces*! A splash of half-and-half (or cream) at the end of cooking puts the whole thing over the top. The resulting dish is tender, creamy, and bursting with fresh vegetable flavor. It's a one-pan pasta treat!

2 tablespoons extra virgin olive oil

½ yellow onion, thinly sliced

2 cloves garlic, thinly sliced

½ pound cremini mushrooms, sliced (about 2 cups)

⅛ teaspoon crushed red pepper

1 teaspoon kosher salt

½ teaspoon ground black pepper

3½ cups vegetable broth

1 bunch asparagus, tough ends trimmed, cut into 1-inch pieces

8 ounces linguine, broken in half

1 cup frozen peas

½ cup chopped scallions, white and light green parts only

½ cup half-and-half or heavy cream

½ cup grated Parmesan cheese, plus more for serving

1 Preheat the oven to 425°F, with a rack in the center position.

2 Heat the olive oil in a medium (5- to 6-quart) Dutch oven over medium-high heat. When the oil is shimmering, add the onion, garlic, and mushrooms and sauté until softened and beginning to brown, about 10 minutes. Stir in the crushed red pepper, salt, and black pepper.

3 Add the broth, asparagus, and linguine and bring to a boil. Immediately cover the pot and transfer it to the oven. Bake until just cooked through, about 20 minutes.

4 Stir in the peas, scallions, half-and-half, and Parmesan and serve the pasta hot, with extra Parmesan cheese for serving.

ULTIMATE OVEN MAC & CHEESE

> SERVES 4 TO 6

1 tablespoon butter

15 ounces whole-milk ricotta cheese

2 teaspoons mustard powder

1 teaspoon garlic powder

¼ teaspoon ground nutmeg

¾ teaspoon kosher salt

¼ teaspoon ground black pepper

4 cups whole milk

2 cups grated sharp cheddar cheese (about 8 ounces)

2 cups grated Gruyère cheese (about 8 ounces)

2 cups grated Parmesan cheese (about 8 ounces)

1 pound pasta shells (uncooked)

1½ cups frozen peas

WHAT MAKES THIS VERSION OF MAC 'N' CHEESE ultimate? Well, for starters, we're using not two, not three, but *four* different kinds of cheese. And that's not even the best part. The best part is that we don't have to bother precooking our pasta shells! The dried pasta soaks up the cheesy sauce right in the pot, coming out tender (and cheese-laden) straight from the oven. I like to add peas, because I'm a bit of a buzzkill, but those are optional, if you want to know the truth. It's a no-fuss kind of one pan wonder, saddled with cheese on cheese (on cheese . . . on cheese). You should probably drop everything and just make this right now.

1 Preheat the oven to 375°F, with a rack in the center position. Grease a medium (5- to 6-quart) Dutch oven with the butter.

2 In a blender, combine the ricotta cheese, mustard powder, garlic powder, nutmeg, salt, and pepper and pulse until very smooth. Slowly add the milk, blending to combine.

3 In the prepared Dutch oven, mix together the grated cheeses. Measure out ½ cup of the mixture and set aside. Stir the ricotta-milk mixture into the cheeses remaining in the pot. Stir in the pasta shells.

4 Cover the pot, transfer to the oven, and bake until the shells are just cooked, 45 minutes to 1 hour, stirring halfway through.

5 Remove the pan from the oven and stir in the peas. Sprinkle the reserved cheese on top. Return to the oven, uncovered, and bake until heated through and the top layer of cheese is browned and bubbling, about 10 minutes.

6 Serve hot.

CHAPTER FOUR

POULTRY

Easy Jerk Chicken with Peppers & Pineapple 115

Warm Kale Caesar with Chicken 122

Roast Turkey Breast with Autumn Veggies 126

Asian Turkey Burgers with Sugar Snaps 133

Cashew Chicken & Veggies 134

Turkey Parm Meatballs with Polenta 141

Green Chicken Chili 116

French Chicken Stew 130

Braised Chicken with Leeks & Tarragon 137

Octavia's Fresh Veggie Soup with Chicken & Feta 138

Easy Chicken Tikka Masala 142

Turkey Sausage, Eggplant & Tomato Penne 143

Thai Turkey with Carrot "Noodles" 119

Saffron Chicken & Rice 120

Quick Chicken Pot Pie 123

Lemon Chicken with Olives & Herbs 146

Chicken Marsala 127

Apricot Glazed Drumsticks with Quinoa 128

Simple Chicken Cassoulet 145

EASY JERK CHICKEN WITH PEPPERS & PINEAPPLE

⊰ SERVES 4 TO 6 ⊱

THIS VERSION OF SPICY, SWEET JAMAICAN JERK chicken may not be perfectly authentic, but it's perfectly delicious and cooks in about 12 minutes under the broiler. The chicken gets charred and juicy, the onion, bell peppers, and fresh pineapple soak up the simple jerk seasonings, and everyone leaves happy. Whether served straight from the pan, over piles of steamed rice, or even tucked inside soft rolls for jerk chicken sandwiches, this is one simple, flavorful recipe for your weeknight arsenal.

1 tablespoon dried thyme

2 teaspoons sugar

1 teaspoon ground allspice

1 teaspoon garlic powder

1 teaspoon kosher salt

¼ teaspoon cayenne pepper

¼ teaspoon ground black pepper

2 bell peppers (I like to use a mix of colors, like red and orange), cut into ½-inch-wide strips

½ fresh pineapple, cored and cut into ½-inch-thick rings

½ yellow onion, cut into ½-inch chunks

3 tablespoons extra virgin olive oil

4 to 6 thin-cut boneless skinless chicken breasts (1 to 1½ pounds total)

1   Preheat the oven to broil, with a rack 4 inches from the heat. Line a sheet pan with foil or mist with cooking spray.

2   To make the jerk seasoning, in a small bowl, whisk together the thyme, sugar, allspice, garlic powder, salt, cayenne, and black pepper.

3   Toss the bell peppers, pineapple, and onion on the prepared pan with the olive oil and a generous pinch of the jerk seasoning, spreading everything out evenly on the pan.

4   Rub the chicken pieces with the remaining jerk seasoning, coating lightly. Nestle the chicken pieces among the vegetables on the pan. Transfer to the oven and broil until the chicken is cooked through and the peppers and pineapple are well charred, 10 to 12 minutes, flipping the chicken halfway through. Keep a close eye on the pan to prevent burning.

5   Serve the chicken and vegetables hot from the oven.

GREEN CHICKEN CHILI

◦ SERVES 4 TO 6 ◦

THIS HANDSOMELY FLAVORED CHILI IS BOTH light and substantial. Fortified with beans, spices, shredded chicken, fresh herbs, and a full can of beer, it's definitely chili at heart, though perhaps more refined, somehow. I mean, we'll definitely go ahead and corrupt it with too much sour cream and fistfuls of chips at serving time, but the underlying air of sophistication will remain. Though roasting your own chicken breasts is a fairly simple task, if you're up for it, shredding the meat off a store-bought rotisserie chicken makes the quickest work of this rich, flavorful stew.

2 tablespoons extra virgin olive oil

2 large yellow onions, chopped

4 cloves garlic, finely chopped

2 (4-ounce) cans chopped mild green chiles

2 teaspoons ground cumin

2 teaspoons dried oregano

½ teaspoon ground cloves

¼ teaspoon chili powder

¼ teaspoon cayenne pepper

½ teaspoon kosher salt

2 (15-ounce) cans Great Northern beans, drained and rinsed

1 (15-ounce) can pinto beans, drained and rinsed

8 cups chicken broth

1 (12-ounce) can beer (I use a lager or pilsner)

3 cups shredded cooked chicken

3 scallions, white and light green parts only, finely chopped

¼ cup chopped fresh cilantro

2 tablespoons chopped fresh basil

Sour cream and chips, for serving (optional)

1 Preheat the oven to 450°F, with a rack in the center position.

2 Heat the olive oil in a medium (5- to 6-quart) Dutch oven over medium-high heat. When the oil is shimmering, add the onions and sauté until softened and starting to brown, about 10 minutes. Stir in the garlic, green chiles, cumin, oregano, cloves, chili powder, cayenne, and salt and cook for 5 minutes more, until fragrant.

3 Add the two types of beans, broth, and beer and bring the chili to a boil. Carefully transfer the pot, uncovered, to the oven and bake until the liquid has reduced by an inch or so, about 30 minutes.

4 Remove the pan from the oven and stir in the chicken. Return to the oven, uncovered, and bake until the chicken is warmed through and the chili reaches your desired thickness, 10 to 20 minutes longer.

5 Stir in the scallions, cilantro, and basil and serve the chili warm, with plenty of toppings alongside, if you like.

THAI TURKEY

WITH

CARROT "NOODLES"

⊰ SERVES 2 TO 4 ⊱

IN THIS ONE-SKILLET SENSATION, TENDER ground turkey is cooked in a flavorful bath of garlic-and-ginger-spiced coconut milk, and some fresh carrot ribbons are tossed in to help soak up the sweet, spicy, salty sauce. A healthy hit of lime juice and some fresh cilantro are the perfect finish. I find this dish great on its own, but it's also fantastic served over rice, rice noodles, or some thinly sliced cabbage, or spooned into lettuce cups. (Note: If you go the lettuce cup route, omit the chicken broth.) You could easily make this whole dish right on the stovetop, but I like to finish it in the oven for that "out of sight, out of mind, now I can clean up the kitchen" mental state.

1 tablespoon canola oil

1¼ pounds ground turkey (I like to use 93% lean)

2 shallots, thinly sliced (about 1 cup)

1 (1-inch) piece fresh ginger, grated (about 2 teaspoons)

2 cloves garlic, minced

4 medium carrots, spiralized (about 2 packed cups; see tip, page 96)

2 tablespoons less-sodium soy sauce

1 cup coconut milk

⅓ cup low-sodium chicken broth

1 teaspoon Sriracha sauce

¼ cup chopped fresh cilantro, plus more for garnish

Juice of ½ lime (about 2 tablespoons)

1 Preheat the oven to 375°F, with a rack in the center position.

2 Heat the oil in a 10-inch cast iron skillet over medium-high heat. When the oil is shimmering, add the turkey and brown well, stirring to break up any larger pieces.

3 Add the shallots, ginger, garlic, and carrot noodles, stirring to incorporate. Stir in the soy sauce, coconut milk, broth, and Sriracha.

4 Carefully transfer the pan to the oven and bake until the carrots are tender and some of the liquid has evaporated, about 10 minutes.

5 Stir in the cilantro and lime juice and serve the turkey hot from the oven, with a sprinkling of extra cilantro, if you like.

SAFFRON CHICKEN & RICE

> ⊱ SERVES 4 TO 6 ⊰

THIS SORT OF HYBRID OF SPANISH PAELLA and classic chicken Marbella is a show-stopper in cast iron. We start it on the stovetop and finish it in the oven, and when it's done? The chicken is juicy and crisp-skinned, the rice forms a lovely crust on the bottom of the pan, the saffron is subtle in its warmth and earthiness, and the olives and prunes give little bursts of sweet, briny flavor throughout. Dinner is served!

1 tablespoon extra virgin olive oil

4 to 6 bone-in, skin-on chicken thighs

Kosher salt and ground black pepper

½ teaspoon saffron threads

2 cups low-sodium chicken broth

1 medium onion, chopped (about 2 cups)

2 cloves garlic, minced

1½ cups basmati rice

10 ounces pitted green olives, roughly chopped (about 1 cup)

½ cup pitted prunes (about 20 pieces)

1 cup white wine

¼ cup chopped fresh flat-leaf parsley

1 Preheat the oven to 400°F, with a rack in the center position.

2 Heat the oil in a 10-inch cast iron skillet over medium-high heat. Season the chicken thighs with 1 teaspoon salt and ½ teaspoon pepper. When the oil is shimmering, add them skin-side down and brown, about 5 minutes. Flip the thighs and cook for another minute. Remove the chicken from the pan and set aside on a plate.

3 While the chicken cooks, combine the saffron with the broth in a small cup to let it bloom.

4 Add the onion to the pan and cook until beginning to soften, about 2 minutes. Add the garlic and cook for 1 minute longer. Add the rice, stirring to coat with the oil in the pan. Stir in the olives and prunes. Add the saffron-broth mixture, the wine, and an extra pinch of salt and pepper and stir to combine.

5 Nestle the chicken pieces back into the pan, skin-side up, and carefully transfer the pan to the oven. Roast until the rice is tender and forms a crisp crust, and a thermometer inserted into the thickest part of the chicken reads 165°F, about 35 minutes.

6 Serve the chicken and rice hot from the oven, garnished with the parsley.

WARM KALE CAESAR WITH CHICKEN

SERVES 2 TO 4

THIS RECIPE IS WHAT HAPPENS WHEN YOUR classic chicken Caesar salad gets a face-lift (on a sheet pan, under the broiler, like all good plastic surgery). Making your own Caesar dressing is super easy and definitely worth it, since we'll slather it on everything here: the thin-cut chicken breasts, leafy kale, and crunchy home-made croutons. The whole dish comes together in about 15 quick minutes, so once you start cooking, be ready to feast!

FOR THE DRESSING

½ cup extra virgin olive oil

1 teaspoon anchovy paste

1 teaspoon grated lemon zest

½ cup fresh lemon juice

1 teaspoon Worcestershire sauce

½ shallot, finely chopped (about ¼ cup)

1 clove garlic, minced

FOR THE SALAD

1 bunch lacinato kale, stemmed and roughly chopped (4 to 5 cups)

4 thin-cut boneless, skinless chicken breasts

Kosher salt and ground black pepper

¼ baguette, cut or torn into ¾-inch chunks

¼ cup grated Parmesan cheese

1 Preheat the oven to 400°F, with one rack in the center position and another 4 inches from the broiler. Line a sheet pan with foil or mist with cooking spray.

2 To make the dressing: In a small bowl or jar, whisk or shake together the olive oil, anchovy paste, lemon zest, lemon juice, Worcestershire, shallot, and garlic.

3 To make the salad: Toss the kale with ½ cup of the dressing on the prepared sheet pan and arrange it in an even layer. Nestle the chicken breasts in the kale, sprinkle them with salt and pepper, and drizzle with about 2 tablespoons of the dressing.

4 Bake until the chicken is halfway cooked through, about 10 minutes.

5 While the chicken cooks, toss the bread cubes with ¼ cup of the dressing.

6 Remove the pan from the oven and set the oven to broil. Scatter the bread cubes around the pan, then return the pan to the top rack and broil, watching carefully to prevent burning, until the chicken is cooked through, the kale is dark and crisp, and the bread is brown and crunchy, 2 to 3 minutes. Sprinkle the Parmesan cheese on top and serve hot, with extra dressing alongside.

QUICK CHICKEN POT PIE

SERVES 4

IS THERE ANYTHING MORE SOUL-WARMING THAN homemade chicken pot pie with biscuits on top? (Besides puppies snuggling babies or something, but that seems a harder scene to come by.) Using store-bought rotisserie chicken helps this bubbling, creamy skillet come together in minutes and, though I do think it's worth it to make the simple drop-biscuit dough from scratch, if you want to use store-bought biscuit dough, I won't judge.

FOR THE BISCUITS

1½ cups all-purpose flour

1 tablespoon sugar

2 teaspoons baking powder

½ teaspoon baking soda

1 teaspoon kosher salt

6 tablespoons cold unsalted butter, cut into ¼-inch cubes

¾ cup cold buttermilk

FOR THE POT PIE

4 tablespoons unsalted butter

1 small onion, chopped (about 1 cup)

2 medium carrots, cut into ½-inch pieces (about 1½ cups)

1 medium Yukon Gold potato, cut into ½-inch pieces (about 1 cup)

⅓ cup all-purpose flour

1 cup low-sodium chicken broth

½ cup half-and-half

3 cups shredded cooked chicken (from a rotisserie chicken)

½ cup chopped scallions, white and light green parts only

1 cup frozen peas

¼ cup chopped fresh dill

1 teaspoon kosher salt

Ground black pepper

1 large egg, beaten

1 Preheat the oven to 425°F, with a rack in the center position.

2 To make the biscuits: In a medium bowl, whisk together the flour, sugar, baking powder, baking soda, and salt. Add the cold butter and work it into the flour mixture with the tips of your fingers, until the butter pieces are well incorporated and the mixture is nubbly looking (the butter pieces should range in size from lentils to peas). Add the buttermilk and mix gently until a shaggy dough comes together. Chill the biscuit dough in the refrigerator until ready to top the chicken pot pie.

RECIPE CONTINUES

3 To make the pot pie: Melt the butter in a 10-inch cast iron skillet over medium-high heat. Add the onion, carrots, and potato and sauté until beginning to soften, 5 to 7 minutes. Add the flour and stir constantly to incorporate. The veggie mixture will get thick and clumpy. Slowly add the chicken broth, stirring well to prevent lumps, and bring to a slow simmer. Stir in the half-and-half, chicken, scallions, peas, dill, salt, and ½ teaspoon pepper.

4 Use a 2-inch ice cream scoop to divide the biscuit dough into 8 portions, dropping each over the skillet and spacing them out evenly. Brush the top of each biscuit with beaten egg and sprinkle with a pinch of ground black pepper.

5 Carefully transfer the skillet to the oven and bake until the biscuits are deeply browned and flaky and the chicken filling is hot and bubbling, 20 to 25 minutes.

6 Serve the chicken pot pie hot from the oven.

ROAST TURKEY BREAST
WITH AUTUMN VEGGIES

⤝ SERVES 4 TO 6 ⤞

MY FAMILY'S THANKSGIVING CELEBRATIONS are loud, boisterous, and big, and I wouldn't have it any other way. But there's a case to be made for a smaller, more intimate holiday experience, and if that's your reality, this recipe might be right up your alley. Instead of wrangling a whole turkey, why not roast a tender turkey breast and all of the best autumn veggies together on a single pan? It's all of the flavor of Thanksgiving, but none of the fuss. In fact, why wait for the fourth Thursday in November? We can be thankful for this dish any day.

1 large red onion, cut into 1-inch-thick wedges

2 large carrots, cut into 1-inch chunks

2 parsnips, peeled and cut into 1-inch chunks

4 medium red potatoes, cut into 1-inch chunks

4 fresh sage leaves

½ teaspoon chopped fresh thyme

4 tablespoons extra virgin olive oil

Kosher salt and ground black pepper

1 (4- to 5-pound) bone-in, skin-on turkey breast

1 Preheat the oven to 450°F, with a rack in the center position. Line a sheet pan with foil or mist with cooking spray.

2 Toss the vegetables on the prepared pan with the sage, thyme, 3 tablespoons of the olive oil, and a large pinch each of salt and pepper. Arrange the veggies in an even layer over the pan.

3 Place the turkey breast on top of the vegetables, skin-side up, and rub thoroughly with the remaining 1 tablespoon olive oil. Sprinkle the skin (and underneath the skin, if you like) with more salt and pepper.

4 Slide the pan into the oven and immediately reduce the temperature to 350°F. Roast the turkey, rotating the pan halfway through cooking, until a thermometer inserted into the thickest part of the breast reads 165°F, about 1 hour.

5 Remove the pan from the oven and tent with foil. Allow the meat to rest for 10 minutes before transferring it to a cutting board and slicing it thinly off the bone.

6 Serve the turkey warm, with the roasted vegetables alongside.

CHICKEN
MARSALA

⊱ SERVES 4 ⊰

I LOVE THE GORGEOUS, EARTHY FLAVOR OF true chicken Marsala, but I don't always want to stand over the stove browning the chicken and mushrooms separately, or building the perfect pan sauce. Enter: the one-pan chicken Marsala method! Baking the chicken and mushrooms together in a casserole dish with plenty of garlicky aromatics, dry Marsala wine, and a splash of cream still gives us deep, rich flavor—it just eliminates all of the hassle of the traditional method. If you like more color on your chicken, run the pan under the broiler for a minute or two at the end of the cooking time.

4 tablespoons unsalted butter

¼ cup all-purpose flour

1 tablespoon garlic powder

1 teaspoon kosher salt

4 boneless, skinless chicken breasts (about 1¼ pounds total)

6 cups sliced cremini mushrooms (about ¾ pound)

1 medium shallot, finely chopped

1 clove garlic, finely chopped

2 tablespoons extra virgin olive oil

1 teaspoon dried oregano

½ teaspoon chopped fresh thyme leaves

¾ cup dry Marsala wine

¼ cup heavy cream

¼ cup chopped fresh flat-leaf parsley, for garnish

1 Preheat the oven to 400°F, with a rack in the center position.

2 Place the butter in a 9 × 13-inch baking dish and put the dish in the oven for about 5 minutes, until the butter is melted. Remove the pan from the oven.

3 While the butter melts, in a medium bowl, whisk together the flour, garlic powder, and ½ teaspoon of the salt. Dredge the chicken pieces in the flour mixture, shaking off any excess. Place the chicken pieces in the pan, turning each piece to coat lightly with the melted butter.

4 In a large bowl, toss together the mushrooms, shallot, garlic, and olive oil. Scatter the vegetables around and on top of the chicken. Sprinkle the dish with the oregano, thyme, and remaining ½ teaspoon salt. Drizzle the wine around the pan.

5 Cover the dish with foil and bake until the chicken is almost but not quite cooked through (a thermometer inserted into the thickest piece will read 155° to 160°F), 30 to 40 minutes.

6 Remove the foil, drizzle the cream around the pan, and return to the oven until a thermometer inserted into the thickest piece reads 165°F, 10 to 15 minutes longer. Serve hot, sprinkled with the parsley.

APRICOT-GLAZED
DRUMSTICKS
WITH
QUINOA

⊸ SERVES 4 TO 6 ⊶

SWEET APRICOT JAM, PAIRED WITH SPICY Dijon, Sriracha, garlic, and soy sauce, makes a sticky, finger-licking marinade for succulent chicken drumsticks in this nearly effortless, and wholly nourishing, oven-baked dish. The quinoa cooks right in the pan alongside the chicken, and the scent of it all should be bottled and sold as perfume. (*Eau de apricot chicken?* Okay, maybe not.)

½ cup apricot jam

1 tablespoon Dijon mustard

1 teaspoon Sriracha sauce

1 clove garlic, finely diced

1 tablespoon less-sodium soy sauce

6 chicken drumsticks

1½ cups quinoa, rinsed

2½ cups chicken broth

1 shallot, finely chopped (about ¼ cup)

1 tablespoon extra virgin olive oil

Kosher salt

½ cup chopped scallions, white and light green parts only

2 tablespoons chopped fresh cilantro

1 Preheat the oven to 375°F, with a rack in the center position.

2 In a large bowl, whisk together the apricot jam, mustard, Sriracha, garlic, and soy sauce until combined. Measure out 3 tablespoons of the marinade and set aside in a small bowl. Place the drumsticks in the large bowl with the rest of the marinade, turning to coat. Set aside to marinate while you prepare the rest of the dish.

3 Stir together the quinoa, broth, shallot, olive oil, and a pinch of salt in a 9 × 13-inch baking dish (or large oval baking dish). Add the chicken drumsticks (with their marinade) to the quinoa, spacing them evenly apart.

4 Transfer to the oven and bake, uncovered, for 20 minutes, then gently stir the quinoa around the pan with a fork to help distribute the moisture in the pan evenly. Continue baking until the quinoa is tender and a thermometer inserted into the thickest drumstick reads 165°F, 20 to 30 minutes longer.

5 Serve hot topped with the scallions and cilantro, with the reserved sauce alongside for drizzling.

FRENCH CHICKEN STEW

⊰ SERVES 4 TO 6 ⊱

THIS IS ONE OF THE MORE INVOLVED RECIPES in the one-pan bunch—we'll brown the bacon and chicken separately before adding them back to the pot and finishing the stew—but it's all in the name of depth of flavor (and *boy,* does this stew have that), plus there's plenty of wine involved here, too, so I feel like it's okay? I mean, a little wine, a little extra time—that's just the French way, *non*? I like to use a few different kinds of chicken pieces in this stew to satisfy everyone at my table—a mix of breasts, thighs, and drumsticks is always appreciated.

6 ounces thick-cut bacon, cut into ½-inch lardons

3 tablespoons extra virgin olive oil

4½ pounds bone-in, skin-on chicken pieces

1 teaspoon kosher salt

½ teaspoon ground black pepper

1 pound cremini mushrooms, sliced (about 3 cups)

1 large red onion, cut into ½-inch-thick wedges (about 3 cups)

4 medium carrots, peeled and cut on an angle into ½-inch pieces (about 2 cups)

3 cloves garlic, finely chopped

2 tablespoons tomato paste

¼ cup all-purpose flour

2 cups dry red wine (I like to use Burgundy)

2 cups chicken broth

5 or 6 fresh thyme sprigs

1 fresh rosemary sprig

¼ cup chopped fresh flat-leaf parsley

1 Preheat the oven to 325°F, with a rack in the center position.

2 Crisp the bacon in a medium (5- to 6-quart) Dutch oven over medium-high heat. When it is browned and the fat is rendered, remove the bacon with tongs or a slotted spoon and transfer to a plate lined with paper towels to drain.

3 Pour off all but 1 tablespoon of bacon fat from the pan and add 2 tablespoons of the olive oil. Season the chicken with the salt and pepper. Still working over medium-high heat, add the chicken pieces, skin-side down, and cook until crisp and golden on all sides, about 10 minutes. Remove the chicken from the pan and set aside on a plate to rest.

4 Add the mushrooms to the pan and cook, stirring occasionally, until they release most of their liquid and start to brown. Add the onion and carrots and cook until just beginning to soften, about 5 minutes. Add the garlic and tomato paste, stirring well to combine, and cook for 1 minute. Stir in the flour and cook for another minute—the mixture will become quite thick, but keep stirring. Stir in the wine and broth, using the spoon to scrape up the browned bits on the bottom of the pan.

5 Nestle the chicken pieces into the liquid, skin-side up. Tie the thyme sprigs and rosemary together with kitchen string and add them, too. Bring the stew to a simmer, then cover and transfer the pot to the oven. Roast until the chicken is tender and a thermometer inserted into the thickest part of the thickest piece of chicken reads 165°F, about 40 minutes. Remove the herb bundle from the pot and discard.

6 Serve hot, topped with the crisp bacon and chopped parsley.

ASIAN TURKEY BURGERS WITH SUGAR SNAPS

SERVES 4

THIS MIGHT COME AS A SHOCK TO SOME, BUT I'm afraid it's true: Turkey burgers don't *have* to be dry, bland hockey pucks on a bun. Spread the word! Roasting the burgers on a wire rack set over a sheet pan (a sheet pan filled with sesame sugar snap peas, mind you) helps them retain moisture; and packing them with garlic, ginger, soy sauce, bell pepper, and spices doesn't hurt, either. The juicy burgers feel extra special served on soft, toasted buns and slathered with a quick-to-come-together spicy avocado mayo. So, yes—it's time to rethink your burger game.

1 pound sugar snap peas (about 4 cups)

1 tablespoon sesame seeds

1 tablespoon plus 1 teaspoon toasted sesame oil

2 tablespoons extra virgin olive oil

¼ teaspoon kosher salt

1 pound ground dark meat turkey

½ cup finely chopped red bell pepper

2 cloves garlic, minced

1 (1-inch) piece fresh ginger, grated (about 2 teaspoons)

2 tablespoons less-sodium soy sauce

Pinch of crushed red pepper

½ cup chopped fresh cilantro

4 hamburger buns, split

½ cup mayonnaise

1 avocado, mashed

2 tablespoons Sriracha sauce

1 Preheat the oven to 400°F, with a rack in the center position. Line a sheet pan with foil.

2 Toss the snap peas with the sesame seeds, 1 tablespoon of the sesame oil, the olive oil, and the salt on the prepared pan. Arrange them in an even layer, then place a well-greased wire rack on top.

3 In a medium bowl, combine the ground turkey, bell pepper, garlic, ginger, soy sauce, crushed red pepper, remaining 1 teaspoon sesame oil, and ¼ cup of the cilantro and mix with your hands. Working gently (resist the urge to squeeze and pack tightly), form the mixture into 4 patties, each about 1½ inches thick.

4 Place the burgers on the wire rack and bake until the snap peas are crisp-tender and a thermometer inserted into the thickest burger reads 165°F, 25 to 30 minutes. Toward the end of cooking, place the buns in the oven, cut-sides down (no pan necessary), to warm through.

5 While the burgers roast, in a medium bowl, whisk together the mayonnaise, mashed avocado, Sriracha, and remaining ¼ cup cilantro.

6 Serve the burgers and buns with dollops of the spicy avocado mayo and snap peas alongside.

CASHEW CHICKEN & VEGGIES

SERVES 4

MY HUSBAND INHERITED HIS LOVE OF CASHEW chicken (that deliciously greasy Chinese food take-out staple) from his father, so for the sake of these two men, I felt it my duty to perfect a (healthier!) one-pan, hands-off version. It turns out that cashew chicken is pretty simple fare—a quick pantry sauce, some sliced veggies, a few thin-cut chicken breasts; give it a turn under the broiler and boom! Cashew chicken for all (and a husband and father-in-law who love you).

½ cup less-sodium soy sauce

¼ cup vegetable oil

2 tablespoons oyster sauce

2 tablespoons toasted sesame oil

1 tablespoon rice vinegar

1 tablespoon packed dark brown sugar

1 tablespoon minced fresh ginger

2 cloves garlic, minced

1 red bell pepper, cut into ½-inch squares

2 large carrots, peeled and cut into very thin (¼-inch) rounds

1 (8-ounce) can sliced water chestnuts, drained

4 to 6 thin-cut boneless skinless chicken breasts (1 to 1½ pounds total)

½ cup roasted salted cashews

3 scallions, white and light green parts only, thinly sliced

2 tablespoons chopped fresh cilantro

1   Preheat the oven to broil, with a rack 4 inches from the heat. Line a sheet pan with foil or mist with cooking spray.

2   In a small bowl, whisk together the soy sauce, vegetable oil, oyster sauce, sesame oil, rice vinegar, brown sugar, ginger, and garlic until well combined.

3   Toss the bell pepper, carrots, and water chestnuts on the prepared pan with half of the sauce, spreading everything out evenly.

4   Place the chicken cutlets among the vegetables and drizzle with the remaining sauce, turning to coat. Transfer the pan to the oven and broil until the chicken is just cooked through and the vegetables are well charred, 10 to 12 minutes, flipping the chicken halfway through. Keep a close eye on the pan to prevent burning. In the last 30 seconds of cooking, toss the cashews onto the pan just to warm up and brown further.

5   Serve the cashew chicken hot from the oven, sprinkled generously with the scallions and cilantro.

BRASED
CHICKEN
WITH
LEEKS &
TARRAGON

SERVES 4

SWEET LEEKS AND AROMATIC TARRAGON ARE the stars of this elegant, Dutch-oven dish. We'll braise them, and some chicken breasts, too, in garlic, ginger, and lemon-infused coconut milk, which serves as a rich and velvety base. A quick pot of rice or loaf of crusty bread on the side helps to soak up the fragrant liquid that graces the bottom of the pan, which is not to be missed.

2 tablespoons extra virgin olive oil

4 bone-in, skin-on chicken breasts

Kosher salt and ground black pepper

2 medium leeks, white and light green parts only, sliced into half-moons and cleaned well (see tip below)

2 cloves garlic, minced

1 (1-inch) piece fresh ginger, grated (about 2 teaspoons)

1 teaspoon grated lemon zest

1 cup chicken broth

1 (13.5-ounce) can coconut milk (see tip, page 84)

2 tablespoons chopped fresh tarragon, plus more for garnish

3 scallions, white and light green parts only, chopped

1 Preheat the oven to 350°F, with a rack in the center position.

2 Heat the olive oil in a medium (5- to 6-quart) Dutch oven over medium-high heat. Sprinkle the chicken with a pinch each salt and pepper. When the oil is shimmering, add the chicken, skin-side down, and sear, without moving, until the pieces pull away easily from the bottom of the pan, 5 to 7 minutes. Flip the chicken and add the leeks, garlic, ginger, lemon zest, 1 teaspoon salt, and ½ teaspoon pepper, stirring to incorporate. Cook for 3 minutes, then add the broth, coconut milk, and tarragon.

3 Cover the pot, slide it into the oven, and bake until a thermometer inserted into the thickest part of the chicken reads 165°F, 30 to 40 minutes.

4 Serve hot, sprinkled with the scallions and some extra tarragon.

HOW TO?
CLEAN LEEKS

I love the delicate, oniony flavor of leeks, but it's important to clean them really well, since they trap grit and sand as they grow. To avoid mouthfuls of dirt (yum!) in your dinner, rinse leeks thoroughly before slicing, then place them in a large bowl of cool water and agitate them gently with your hand to release any sand or dirt. Allow the leeks to sit in the water for a few minutes while the sand sinks to the bottom of the bowl. Gently scoop the clean leeks out of the water. Pat them dry with a clean kitchen towel or paper towel, and enjoy your dirt-free meal!

OCTAVIA'S FRESH VEGGIE SOUP
WITH CHICKEN & FETA

> SERVES 4 TO 6

MY MOTHER-IN-LAW, OCTAVIA, IS ONE OF those effortless cooks, the kind who greets you at the door with a glass of wine, then sails around the kitchen chatting with interest and suddenly— voilà! She has turned out a beautifully prepared, unpretentious but stylish meal. This soup recipe is hers and, true to form, it's both unassuming (a simple vegetable-based soup with shredded chicken mixed in) and remarkable. Lots of fennel, some white wine, and a crumble of feta help with the remarkable part—it's a soup with character, with zip, with panache—sort of like Octavia herself.

3 tablespoons extra virgin olive oil

2 onions, finely chopped

5 cloves garlic, minced

½ teaspoon dried oregano

¼ teaspoon crushed red pepper

½ teaspoon kosher salt

¼ teaspoon ground black pepper

1 cup white wine

1 (14.5-ounce) can diced tomatoes with juice

6 cups chicken broth

2 medium bulbs fennel, cored and thinly sliced

2 medium zucchini, chopped

1 yellow bell pepper, chopped

⅓ cup orzo

2 cups shredded cooked chicken

¼ cup chopped fresh flat-leaf parsley

½ cup crumbled feta cheese

1 Heat the olive oil in a medium (5- to 6-quart) Dutch oven over medium-high heat. When the oil is shimmering, add the onions and sauté until just beginning to brown, 5 to 7 minutes. Add the garlic, oregano, crushed red pepper, salt, and black pepper and sauté for another minute or two, until fragrant.

2 Add the wine and bring to a boil. Stir in the tomatoes, broth, fennel, zucchini, and bell pepper, reduce the heat, and simmer the soup for 20 minutes.

3 Add the orzo, chicken, and parsley and cook until the orzo is tender and the chicken is warmed through, 10 minutes longer. Taste the soup and adjust the seasonings as you like.

4 Serve the soup hot, topped with the crumbled feta.

TURKEY PARM
MEATBALLS
WITH
POLENTA

ROASTING TURKEY MEATBALLS IN THE OVEN is a revelation—they turn out moist and juicy and, unlike when you cook them in a pot on the stove, you don't have to worry that they'll fall apart as you nudge and flip them to get them to brown on all sides. Just break out your sheet pan! Because turkey meatballs roasted over creamy polenta and topped with marinara sauce and fresh mozzarella? Revelatory.

1 (24-ounce) log precooked polenta, sliced into ½-inch-thick rounds

Kosher salt and ground black pepper

1 small yellow onion

1½ pounds ground turkey (dark meat is best)

1 tablespoon tomato paste

¼ cup Italian-style bread crumbs

1 cup grated Parmesan cheese (4 ounces)

1½ teaspoons dried oregano

3½ cups (36 ounces) store-bought marinara sauce (I like Rao's)

¾ pound fresh mozzarella cheese, thinly sliced

¼ cup chopped or chiffonade-cut fresh basil (see tip, page 83)

1   Preheat the oven to 400°F, with a rack in the center position. Line a sheet pan with foil or mist with cooking spray.

2   Arrange the polenta rounds on the prepared pan and sprinkle each of them with a pinch each of salt and pepper.

3   Using the large holes on a box grater, grate the onion into a large bowl, catching any juice that accumulates. Add the ground turkey, tomato paste, bread crumbs, Parmesan, oregano, and 1 teaspoon salt and use your hands to combine. Working gently to avoid tough meatballs (resist the urge to squeeze and pack tightly), form the meat mixture into 1½-inch meatballs.

4   Place the meatballs around and on top of the polenta on the sheet pan, and mist them with cooking spray. Bake the polenta and meatballs until a thermometer inserted into the biggest meatball reads 165°F, about 20 minutes, flipping the meatballs halfway through.

5   Remove from the oven, spoon the marinara sauce on top of the meatballs, and lay the fresh mozzarella on top of the sauce. Return to the oven and bake until the sauce is hot and the cheese is melted, 10 minutes longer.

6   Serve hot, sprinkled with basil.

EASY
CHICKEN TIKKA MASALA

⊱ SERVES 4 TO 6 ⊰

2 pounds boneless, skinless chicken thighs, cut into 1-inch pieces

½ cup plain Greek yogurt (I like full fat)

2 tablespoons unsalted butter

2 tablespoons extra virgin olive oil

1 large yellow onion, finely chopped

4 cloves garlic, minced

1 (1-inch) piece fresh ginger, grated

2 tablespoons garam masala

2 teaspoons hot or smoked paprika

2 teaspoons kosher salt

2 tablespoons tomato paste

1 (28-ounce) can diced tomatoes

½ cup heavy cream or coconut milk

Cooked rice, for serving

¼ cup chopped fresh cilantro, for garnish

GROWING UP IN A LESS THAN ADVENTUROUS eating household, I didn't try Indian food until college, where I took one bite of chicken tikka masala and was promptly hooked. Sticking true to my upbringing, it took me a while to try anything other than chicken tikka, but I slowly branched out and learned to enjoy curries, naans, tandoori-grilled meats, and pretty much anything involving paneer. Still, I often fall back on my old chicken tikka standby—it's just so buttery, so heartwarming, so good! This simple, one-pot version is one I promise you'll want to eat over and over again, too. If you have time, it's best to marinate the chicken overnight, but a quick, 20-minute marinade bath works, too. The chicken cooks low and slow—for about 4 hours—in the oven, which is definitely a time commitment, but the tender, melt-in-your-mouth results are so worth it.

1 Place the chicken pieces and yogurt in a zip-top bag or sealable container and turn to coat. Marinate in the refrigerator for about 6 hours, or overnight (you can skip this step if you don't have time).

2 Preheat the oven to 300°F, with a rack in the center position.

3 Melt the butter in the olive oil in a medium (5- to 6-quart) Dutch oven over medium-high heat. Add the onion and sauté until just beginning to brown. Add the garlic and ginger and sauté for another minute or two, then add the garam masala, paprika, and salt, stirring to incorporate and toast the spices.

4 Stir in the tomato paste and diced tomatoes, then add the marinated chicken (with any yogurt marinade), stirring until everything is well mixed.

5 Cover and bake until the chicken is cooked through and very tender, about 4 hours.

6 In the last 15 minutes of cooking, stir in the heavy cream. (If you want the sauce to be thicker, leave the cover off for those last 15 minutes.)

7 Serve the chicken tikka masala hot from the oven, over a pile of rice and topped with cilantro.

TURKEY SAUSAGE, EGGPLANT & TOMATO PENNE

SERVES 4

WHEN I WAS A KID, YOU COULDN'T PAY ME to eat eggplant. Mostly, it was just confusing—it's not eggs, is it? With a shape like that, are we sure it's even a plant? Now, of course, I can't get enough of the sweet, almost creamy vegetable. In this one-pot pasta marvel, dried penne cooks to perfection with meaty turkey sausage, bright marinara sauce, and plenty of velvety, sautéed eggplant. Smothered with fresh basil and Parmesan cheese, this is a dish I think nine-year-old me might even go for.

3 tablespoons extra virgin olive oil

1 eggplant, cut into 1-inch cubes

½ teaspoon kosher salt

¼ teaspoon ground black pepper

2 cloves garlic, minced

1 pound turkey sausage, casings removed

2 cups chicken broth

12 ounces penne pasta (about 3 cups)

2 cups store-bought marinara sauce (I like Rao's)

¼ cup chopped or chiffonade-cut fresh basil (see tip, page 83)

Grated Parmesan cheese, for topping

1   Preheat the oven to 425°F, with a rack in the center position.

2   Heat the olive oil in a medium (5- to 6-quart) Dutch oven over medium-high heat. When the oil is shimmering, add the eggplant and sauté until golden brown, about 10 minutes. Add the salt, pepper, and garlic and sauté for another minute or two, until fragrant. Use tongs or a slotted spoon to scoop the eggplant out of the pot and set it aside in a medium bowl.

3   Add the turkey sausage to the pot, breaking it up with a wooden spoon or spatula, and cook until well browned, about 10 minutes. Add the broth, pasta, and marinara sauce, and stir well.

4   Bring the mixture to a boil. Cover, carefully transfer to the oven, and bake until the pasta is just cooked through, about 20 minutes. Remove from the oven and stir in the cooked eggplant.

5   Serve hot, sprinkled with the basil and Parmesan.

SIMPLE CHICKEN CASSOULET

CASSOULET IS CLASSIC FRENCH COMFORT food. There are a million ways to make it, but most recipes are a bit, uh, involved (read: one thousand ingredients, seven pages long, probably including steps to confit your own duck legs . . .). I figured we could make a version of cassoulet that's just as hearty, just as satisfying, but entirely fuss free. Baking chicken drumsticks with precooked sausages, plenty of aromatics, and a bit of white wine does the trick, and a crunchy panko topping seals the deal—this may not be an authentic cassoulet, but look! Everyone's too busy enjoying dinner to notice.

6 chicken drumsticks

Kosher salt and ground black pepper

4 cooked sweet Italian-style chicken sausages (3 ounces each), halved on a diagonal

½ yellow onion, chopped (about 1 cup)

3 small carrots, cut into ½-inch slices (about 1 cup)

4 tablespoons extra virgin olive oil

1 (15½-ounce) can white beans, drained and rinsed

1 clove garlic, thinly sliced

5 or 6 fresh thyme sprigs

½ cup white wine

½ cup low-sodium chicken broth

1 cup panko bread crumbs

1 tablespoon grated lemon zest

3 tablespoons chopped fresh flat-leaf parsley

1 Preheat the oven to 375°F, with one rack in the center position and another 4 inches from the broiler.

2 Arrange the chicken in the bottom of a 9 × 13-inch baking dish and season with salt and pepper. Place the sausages around the drumsticks and scatter the onion and carrots all over. Drizzle everything with 2 tablespoons of the olive oil, then arrange the beans, garlic, and thyme sprigs evenly around the pan. Drizzle over the wine and broth.

3 Bake on the center rack until the dish is fragrant and a thermometer inserted into the thickest drumstick reads 165°F, 45 to 55 minutes.

4 While the chicken cooks, in a medium bowl, mix the panko, lemon zest, parsley, remaining 2 tablespoons olive oil, and a pinch each of salt and pepper.

5 Remove the dish from the oven and set the oven to broil. Top the cassoulet thickly with the panko mixture and return to the oven to broil until the panko topping is golden brown and crisp, about 1 minute.

6 Serve hot.

LEMON CHICKEN

WITH

OLIVES & HERBS

⊱ SERVES 2 TO 4 ⊰

HERE, PAN-SEARED CHICKEN BREASTS GET tossed with garlic, lemon, white wine, fresh herbs, and chopped olives, and the whole thing finishes spectacularly quickly in the oven. It's bright with lemon, briny with olives, fresh and refined with herbs, and pairs wonderfully with some bread or a green salad alongside.

2 tablespoons extra virgin olive oil

2 to 4 boneless, skinless chicken breasts

½ teaspoon kosher salt

½ teaspoon ground black pepper

2 teaspoons all-purpose flour

2 cloves garlic, minced

½ cup dry white wine

1 teaspoon grated lemon zest

¼ cup fresh lemon juice

1 teaspoon chopped fresh thyme leaves

1 cup chopped pitted green olives

1 tablespoon chopped fresh dill

1 tablespoon chopped fresh flat-leaf parsley

1 Preheat the oven to 400°F, with a rack in the center position.

2 Heat the oil in a 10-inch cast iron skillet over medium-high heat. Season the chicken with the salt and pepper and sprinkle them with the flour. When the oil is shimmering, add the chicken and sear until well browned all over, about 3 minutes per side.

3 Add the garlic, wine, lemon zest, lemon juice, thyme, and olives. Transfer the pan to the oven and bake until a thermometer inserted into the thickest part of a breast reads 165°F, about 10 minutes.

4 Serve hot, topped with fresh dill and parsley.

CHAPTER FIVE

FISH

SEA BASS
WITH
FRESH CORN SUCCOTASH

SERVES 4

SUFFERIN' SUCCOTASH! THIS ONE'S A BEAUT.
Our lovely fish fillets roast together on a sheet pan with a crisp, colorful mess of fresh corn, red onion, sweet tomatoes, and edamame. Topped with lots of fresh basil, it's a bright, summery dish made for a bright, summery day. If you can't find sea bass, feel free to substitute halibut, sablefish, or cod.

4 (5- to 6-ounce) sea bass fillets

Kosher salt and ground black pepper

4 tablespoons unsalted butter

4 ears corn, kernels sliced from the cobs

2 cups frozen shelled edamame, thawed and patted dry

1 medium red onion, chopped

½ cup cherry or grape tomatoes, halved

½ teaspoon grated lemon zest

2 tablespoons extra virgin olive oil

¼ cup chopped or chiffonade-cut fresh basil (see tip, page 83)

1   Preheat the oven to 350°F, with a rack in the center position. Line a sheet pan with parchment paper or mist with cooking spray.

2   Arrange the fish fillets on the prepared pan and top each one with a pinch of salt and 1 tablespoon of the butter.

3   In a large bowl, toss together the corn, edamame, onion, tomatoes, lemon zest, olive oil, and a pinch each of salt and pepper. Arrange the corn succotash around the fish fillets on the pan.

4   Bake until the vegetables are tender but still bright and the fish is opaque and flaky, 20 to 30 minutes.

5   Serve warm, sprinkled with basil.

ROASTED
SHRIMP
& CHICKPEA
SALAD

> ⊶ SERVES 2 TO 4 ⊷

THIS QUICK SALAD IS A WONDERFUL MIX OF texture, temperature, and flavor. The shrimp, chickpeas, and red onion roast together on a sheet pan with a quickly made lemony vinaigrette, getting plump and juicy and warm. Then we stir in some crisp celery and fresh dill to add coolness and crunch. It's an unexpectedly fun and healthy treat, whether dished up for dinner or boxed up and toted to work as a "not sad desk lunch." Serve with a few slices of crusty baguette.

1 pound peeled and deveined large shrimp, tails removed

1 (15-ounce) can chickpeas, drained and rinsed

1 small red onion, thinly sliced

¼ cup fresh lemon juice, plus more for serving

2 tablespoons capers, drained

¼ cup extra virgin olive oil

¼ teaspoon kosher salt

¼ teaspoon ground black pepper

4 stalks celery, chopped (about 2 cups)

2 tablespoons chopped fresh dill

½ cup chopped fresh flat-leaf parsley

1   Preheat the oven to 400°F, with a rack in the center position.

2   Toss the shrimp, chickpeas, onion, lemon juice, capers, olive oil, salt, and pepper together on a sheet pan. Roast until the shrimp are pink and opaque, about 10 minutes.

3   Remove the pan from the oven. Add the celery, dill, and parsley and stir to combine.

4   Serve the shrimp salad warm or at room temperature, with an extra squeeze of lemon on top.

HALIBUT
WITH
WILTED GREENS & CITRUS SALSA

SERVES 4

WHENEVER WE SEE HALIBUT ON A MENU MY Uncle Bob makes a terrible joke about ordering it "just for the halibut." It's so bad that it's almost good, and we find ourselves in stitches every time. Because get it? Do you get it? . . . Just for the halibut? Okay, yeah, it's just bad. But making halibut at home is a luxury. Fresh fillets can be pricey, so treat them right. A hot cast iron skillet is the perfect vessel for turning out crisp-skinned, moist fillets. Topping them with warm, wilted Swiss chard and cool citrus salsa is definitely the way to go.

4 tablespoons extra virgin olive oil

4 (5-ounce) halibut fillets, pin bones removed (see tip, page 168)

Kosher salt and ground black pepper

1 bunch Swiss chard, washed, dried, and roughly chopped

1 pink grapefruit, suprêmed (see tip below) and chopped

2 navel oranges, suprêmed and chopped

3 scallions, white and light green parts only, thinly sliced

½ medium jalapeño, seeded and diced

1 Preheat the oven to 350°F, with a rack in the center position.

2 Heat 1 tablespoon of the olive oil in a 10-inch cast iron skillet over medium-high heat. When the oil is shimmering, add the halibut fillets skin-side down. Sprinkle the tops with a pinch of salt and sear, without moving, for 4 to 5 minutes.

3 Meanwhile, in a large bowl, combine the chard, 2 tablespoons of the olive oil, and ½ teaspoon salt and toss to coat.

4 Place the chard around and on top of the fish in the pan. Carefully transfer the skillet to the oven and bake until the greens are quite wilted and the fish is opaque and flaky throughout, 15 to 20 minutes.

5 While the fish bakes, make the salsa: In a large bowl, stir together the grapefruit, oranges, scallions, jalapeño, remaining 1 tablespoon olive oil, and a pinch each of salt and black pepper.

6 Serve the fish warm on a bed of the wilted greens, topped with citrus salsa.

HOW TO?
SUPRÊME CITRUS

To suprême citrus means cutting the fruit segments cleanly from the peel and membranes. To do it, just slice off the outer peel and tough, white pith, then use a small knife to wiggle and wedge the individual orange and grapefruit segments from the dividing membranes inside. Voilà! Suprêmed.

INDIAN
SPICED
HADDOCK

⊱ SERVES 4 ⊰

HADDOCK IS A MILD WHITE FISH THAT TENDS to soak up the flavor of whatever it's cooked with, so the warmth of the spices (cumin, turmeric, cinnamon, and chili powder) really shines in this quick, coconut-scented stew. I like serving this one in shallow bowls over a bit of rice or warmed naan bread.

½ teaspoon chili powder

½ teaspoon ground cumin

½ teaspoon ground turmeric

¼ teaspoon ground cinnamon

1 teaspoon kosher salt

4 (5-ounce) skinless haddock fillets

1 tablespoon extra virgin olive oil

½ medium onion, thinly sliced

1 (14½-ounce) can diced tomatoes

1 cup coconut milk (see tip, page 84)

1 tablespoon fresh lemon juice

2 tablespoons chopped fresh cilantro

1 Preheat the oven to 350°F, with a rack in the center position.

2 In a small bowl, mix together the chili powder, cumin, turmeric, cinnamon, and ½ teaspoon of the salt. Season the fish all over with the spice mixture.

3 Heat the oil in a 10-inch cast iron skillet over medium-high heat. When the oil is shimmering, sear the fish for about 3 minutes on one side. Flip the fish and add the onion, tomatoes, coconut milk, and remaining ½ teaspoon salt, stirring the liquid to combine.

4 Transfer the pan to the oven and bake until the fish is opaque and flaky, about 15 minutes.

5 Remove the pan from the oven and squeeze the lemon juice on top. Serve hot, sprinkled with cilantro.

PESTO SNAPPER EN BRODO

SERVES 4

2 tablespoons extra virgin olive oil

1 leek, white and light green parts only, sliced into half-moons and cleaned well (see tip, page 137)

1 clove garlic, minced

½ teaspoon kosher salt

2 tablespoons Pernod

2 cups seafood stock (or vegetable or chicken broth)

4 (5-ounce) red snapper fillets, skinned, pin bones removed (see tip, page 168)

FOR THE PESTO

1 cup packed fresh basil leaves

½ cup walnuts, toasted

1 clove garlic, chopped

1 teaspoon fresh lemon juice

¼ cup extra virgin olive oil

Kosher salt and ground black pepper

COOKING SOMETHING EN BRODO JUST MEANS "in broth," and it makes for both a warmly comforting and humbly elegant presentation. We'll make things easy by fortifying some store-bought broth with leeks, garlic, and a splash of anise-flavored liqueur called Pernod (though if you're fresh out of Pernod, you could easily substitute some dry white wine). I've included a recipe for fresh pesto, but if you'd rather use a cup or so of premade, that will work equally well. And if you can't find red snapper fillets, another mild white fish, such as sole or black sea bass, will do the trick, too.

1   Preheat the oven to 350°F, with a rack in the center position.

2   Heat the olive oil in a 10-inch cast iron skillet over medium-high heat. When the oil is shimmering, add the leek and sauté until soft and beginning to brown, about 5 minutes. Add the garlic and salt and cook for 1 minute more, until fragrant. Add the Pernod and stock to the pan, stirring to scrape up any browned bits from the bottom of the pan, and bring to a simmer.

3   Slide the fish fillets into the broth. Carefully transfer the pan to the oven and bake until the fish is opaque and flaky, about 15 minutes.

4   While the fish bakes, make the pesto: In a food processor, combine the basil, walnuts, garlic, lemon juice, and olive oil and process until smooth. Season with salt and pepper.

5   Serve the fish in shallow bowls, with plenty of broth and fresh pesto ladled on top.

SALMON & HERB
BURGERS
WITH
GARLICKY
ZUCCHINI

SERVES 4

AS A PACIFIC NORTHWESTERNER, I THINK I'M contractually obligated to include a recipe for salmon in this cookbook. Where I live in Seattle, fresh salmon is usually on the menu from spring through fall, and in every application imaginable—baked, roasted, broiled, smoked, stewed, moussed, burgered—how lucky are we? But if you can get your hands on some salmon fillets (and ask the fishmonger to skin them and remove the pin bones for you—and, better yet, chop them into chunks, too), you can enjoy these sweet burgers, bursting with green herbs and briny capers, wherever you are. Paired with thinly sliced, garlicky zucchini, these are fantastic served either atop soft buns (with a smear of mayo or Dijon on top, perhaps) or over a mess of fresh greens.

1½ pounds skinless salmon fillets, cut into 2-inch chunks

½ yellow onion, chopped (about 1 cup)

2 tablespoons Dijon mustard

¼ cup capers, drained

¼ cup chopped fresh dill

¼ cup chopped fresh parsley

2 tablespoons chopped fresh tarragon

1 heaping teaspoon grated lemon zest

½ teaspoon crushed red pepper

1½ medium zucchini, sliced into ½-inch-thick rounds

2 cloves garlic, minced

2 tablespoons extra virgin olive oil

¼ teaspoon kosher salt

¼ teaspoon ground black pepper

Burger buns or fresh greens, for serving

1   Preheat the oven to broil, with a rack about 5 inches from the heat. Mist a sheet pan with cooking spray and spray a wire rack, too.

2   In a food processor, pulse the salmon and onion together about 20 times, until the salmon is roughly chopped but easily clumps together. Transfer the salmon mixture to a medium bowl.

3   Add the mustard, capers, dill, parsley, tarragon, lemon zest, and crushed red pepper to the salmon and use your hands to combine. Working gently (resist the urge to pack tightly), form the mixture into 4 patties. Place the burgers on the prepared wire rack.

4   Toss the zucchini on the prepared sheet pan with the garlic, olive oil, salt, and pepper. Arrange in an even layer. Place the wire rack with the burgers on top of the zucchini layer.

5   Broil the salmon burgers and zucchini until the salmon burgers are tender and cooked to medium, about 10 minutes, flipping the burgers halfway through. If you like your burgers cooked through, keep them in for a few minutes extra.

6   Serve the burgers and zucchini hot from the oven, on burger buns or over fresh greens.

CLAMBAKE IN A POT

⤜ SERVES 4 TO 6 ⤛

WHEN I HEAR THE WORD CLAMBAKE, I THINK warm sand, bare toes, and salty breezes (and maybe popped collars and Nantucket reds, too). It's a nice thought, especially when it's forty-five degrees and raining in Seattle. But even if we can't have the beach, we can still have the clambake! One pot is all it takes to throw together our own landlubber's version. Sausage, corn, and small potatoes are a must—and plenty of seafood, of course. I like using a mix of clams and shrimp, but you could certainly add a handful of mussels or even some lobster pieces if you're so inclined.

2 tablespoons unsalted butter

¼ cup extra virgin olive oil

1 large yellow onion, chopped

14 ounces kielbasa (or other smoked, spicy sausage), cut into 1-inch-thick slices

1 teaspoon kosher salt

½ teaspoon ground black pepper

1 pound small potatoes (red or white)

2 ears corn, husked and cut crosswise into 4 pieces each

2 dozen littleneck clams, scrubbed

1½ pounds shell-on medium shrimp

2 cups dry white wine

3 tablespoons chopped fresh tarragon

1 Preheat the oven to 425°F, with a rack in the center position.

2 Melt the butter in the olive oil in a large (7- to 8-quart) Dutch oven over medium-high heat. Add the onion and sauté until softened and starting to brown, 8 to 10 minutes. Add the kielbasa, salt, and pepper and cook until lightly brown, 10 minutes more.

3 Layer the remaining ingredients in the pot in this order: potatoes, corn, clams, shrimp. Pour the wine on top of everything and bring to a boil.

4 Cover the pot tightly and transfer it to the oven. Bake until the potatoes are tender, the clams have opened, and the shrimp are just pink and cooked through, 25 to 30 minutes.

5 Use a large slotted spoon to scoop out all the veggies, sausage, and seafood goodies into bowls and sprinkle with the tarragon. Discard any clams that haven't opened. Carefully ladle the broth over the seafood, being careful not to scoop out any sand that might have collected in the bottom of the pan.

6 Serve hot.

HONEY-ORANGE
SALMON
& BROCCOLINI

SERVES 4

BROCCOLINI IS A SORT OF LONGER-STEMMED, smaller-headed, perfectly sweet cousin of regular broccoli. Here, the quick-cooking veggie couples nicely with juicy salmon fillets and a heady, piquant sauce laced with honey, orange, and hot sauce. The whole dish cooks in about 20 minutes on a sheet pan, so it's perfect for busy weekends and weeknights alike.

2 teaspoons grated orange zest

¼ cup fresh orange juice

¼ cup plus 1 tablespoon extra virgin olive oil

2 tablespoons honey

1 tablespoon hot sauce (I like Frank's or Cholula)

1 tablespoon Dijon mustard

3 cloves garlic, minced

2 bunches broccolini, cut into ½-inch pieces

Kosher salt

4 (5-ounce) skin-on salmon fillets

1 Preheat the oven to 375°F, with a rack in the center position. Line a sheet pan with foil or mist with cooking spray.

2 In a medium bowl, whisk together the orange zest, orange juice, ¼ cup of the olive oil, the honey, hot sauce, mustard, and garlic until smooth.

3 Toss the broccolini with the remaining 1 tablespoon olive oil and a pinch of salt on the prepared sheet pan. Drizzle half of the marinade over the broccolini and toss again, spreading the broccolini in an even layer around the edges of the pan.

4 Place the salmon fillets in the center of the pan and drizzle with the remaining marinade.

5 Bake until the broccolini is crisp-tender and the salmon is just cooked through, about 20 minutes. Serve hot.

COD

WITH
OLIVES &
CIPOLLINIS
IN
TOMATO
SAUCE

SERVES 4

THIS IS A TRUE *ONE PAN & DONE*—ALL WE have to do is pile the ingredients in a casserole dish, slide it unceremoniously into the oven, and wait for our meal to cook itself to sweet-smelling perfection. Mild, flaky cod is the perfect foil for the brightly acidic sauce of tomato, orange, and dark olives; and little cipollini onions bring a pop of sweetness and spice. If you can't find cipollinis, you can substitute a regular onion or two, sliced into thick wedges.

4 (5-ounce) skinless cod fillets

6 ounces cipollini onions, halved (about 2 cups)

3 tablespoons extra virgin olive oil

1 cup pitted kalamata olives

1 (14.5 ounce) can diced tomatoes

2 plum tomatoes, chopped (about 1 cup)

¼ teaspoon crushed red pepper

1 clove garlic, finely chopped

1 teaspoon grated orange zest

Juice of 1 orange (about ½ cup)

½ teaspoon kosher salt

½ teaspoon chopped fresh thyme

¼ cup chopped or chiffonade-cut fresh basil (see tip, page 83)

1   Preheat the oven to 350°F, with a rack in the center position.

2   Arrange the cod fillets in a single layer in a 9 × 13-inch glass or ceramic baking dish. Scatter the rest of the ingredients, except the basil, over and around the fish.

3   Transfer to the oven and bake until the cod is opaque and flaky and the onions are tender, 25 to 30 minutes.

4   Serve hot, topped with the basil.

GARLIC-BROILED
SCALLOPS
WITH
CHERRY TOMATOES & PANCETTA

⟨ SERVES 2 TO 4 ⟩

THIS IS A SPECIAL-OCCASION KIND OF MEAL on a sheet pan. Sweet, buttery scallops can be a lot of dollar signs, so if you're cooking for a crowd and want to fill out the pan with some shrimp to save cash, I definitely support you. Still, if you can swing it (or if you're just cooking for two, say), this is one fantastic way to cook scallops. We basically just broil them in pancetta drippings, smothered with garlic and joined at the hip with fresh tomatoes, a bit of Parmesan, and handfuls of fresh herbs. The finished dish is salty, sweet, briny, and bright—and did I mention the pancetta drippings?

¾ pound pancetta, cut into ½-inch cubes

10 ounces (about 2 cups) cherry tomatoes

1 to 1½ pounds sea scallops (12 to 16 scallops)

3 tablespoons extra virgin olive oil

4 cloves garlic, finely chopped

1 tablespoon grated Parmesan cheese

2 tablespoons chopped fresh tarragon or flat-leaf parsley

1 Preheat the oven to 400°F, with one rack in the center position and another set about 4 inches from the broiler. Line a sheet pan with foil and mist with cooking spray.

2 Place the pancetta on the prepared sheet pan and bake on the center rack until the fat is rendered and the meat is starting to crisp, about 10 minutes.

3 While the pancetta cooks, toss the tomatoes and scallops in a medium bowl with the olive oil, garlic, and Parmesan.

4 Remove the pancetta from the oven and set the oven to broil. Arrange the tomatoes and scallops in an even layer around the pancetta. Slide the pan under the broiler and broil until the tomatoes are bursting and the scallops are opaque and cooked through, about 2 minutes, flipping the scallops halfway through the cooking.

5 Serve hot, topped with the tarragon or parsley.

TUNA STEAKS

WITH
EDAMAME
& CAPER
VINAIGRETTE

SERVES 4

TUNA STEAKS ARE A SPLURGE, BUT SIMPLY baking them with creamy edamame and topping with a bright, briny caper vinaigrette is definitely worth it. Keep an eye on the fish as it roasts—we want it still pink in the center when it's done, so it stays tender and moist.

4 (5-ounce) sushi-grade tuna steaks, about 1 inch thick

1 (12-ounce) bag frozen shelled edamame, thawed, drained, and patted dry

Kosher salt and ground black pepper

9 tablespoons extra virgin olive oil

5 tablespoons fresh lemon juice

1 teaspoon Dijon mustard

2 tablespoons capers, drained and chopped

2 tablespoons chopped fresh flat-leaf parsley

1 Preheat the oven to 450°F, with a rack in the center position.

2 Arrange the tuna steaks in an even layer in a 9 × 13-inch glass or ceramic baking dish and scatter the edamame around the steaks. Sprinkle the tuna and beans with ½ teaspoon salt and drizzle with 3 tablespoons of the olive oil and 2 tablespoons of the lemon juice.

3 Transfer to the oven and bake until the tuna begins to flake when tested with a fork, but is still pink in the center, about 10 minutes.

4 While the tuna bakes, make the vinaigrette: In a medium bowl, whisk together the remaining 3 tablespoons lemon juice, the mustard, and a pinch each of salt and pepper. Drizzle in the remaining 6 tablespoons olive oil, whisking constantly, until emulsified. Stir in the capers and parsley.

5 Serve the tuna steaks and edamame hot from the oven, with spoonfuls of caper vinaigrette on top.

SESAME-GINGER
SHRIMP
WITH
CHINESE EGGPLANT

SERVES 4

I'VE SAID IT BEFORE AND I'LL SAY IT AGAIN—roasting shrimp is the ultimate move! There's no better way to get juicier, more flavorful little morsels of seafood. Adding creamy eggplant and a sweet, salty, sesame-ginger glaze? Well, fine, maybe that's one better way.

¼ cup rice vinegar

¼ cup extra virgin olive oil

¼ cup toasted sesame oil

1 (2-inch) piece fresh ginger, minced

3 cloves garlic, minced

1 tablespoon packed light brown sugar

2 teaspoons sesame seeds

½ teaspoon crushed red pepper

1 teaspoon kosher salt

2 Chinese eggplants, cut into ¾-inch pieces (about 4 cups)

1½ pounds medium shrimp, peeled and deveined

4 scallions, white and light green parts only, thinly sliced

1 Preheat the oven to 400°F, with a rack in the center position. Line a sheet pan with foil or mist with cooking spray.

2 In a medium bowl, whisk together the vinegar, olive oil, sesame oil, ginger, garlic, brown sugar, sesame seeds, crushed red pepper, and salt until smooth.

3 Toss the eggplant with half of the marinade on the prepared sheet pan to coat, then spread out in an even layer. Transfer to the oven and roast until almost tender, about 15 minutes.

4 Meanwhile, toss the shrimp with the rest of the marinade in the bowl and let sit while the eggplant cooks.

5 Remove the pan from the oven. Add the shrimp and the marinade to the pan, spreading them evenly over the eggplant. Return to the oven and roast until the shrimp are pink and opaque, 8 to 10 minutes more.

6 Serve hot, sprinkled with the scallions.

BAKED SALMON WITH DILLED BREAD CRUMBS

SERVES 4

THOUGH COOKING INDIVIDUAL FILLETS CAN BE nice and tidy, there's something very elegant about roasting a whole side (or large fillet) of fish. Bringing the dish to the table and letting everyone flake off their portion feels special, somehow—particularly if the fish in question is topped with a garlicky, lemon-scented, dill-flecked crust of crispy panko. A simply dressed green salad is the perfect accompaniment to this chic and tasty meal.

1 large salmon fillet (1½ to 2 pounds), pin bones removed (see tip below)

1 cup panko bread crumbs

½ cup chopped fresh dill

1 teaspoon grated lemon zest

1 clove garlic, minced

1 teaspoon kosher salt

1 teaspoon mustard powder

3 tablespoons extra virgin olive oil

1 Preheat the oven to 425°F, with one rack in the center position and another 4 inches from the broiler.

2 Place the salmon fillet in a 9 × 13-inch glass or ceramic baking dish, skin-side down. In a medium bowl, mix together the panko, dill, lemon zest, garlic, salt, mustard powder, and olive oil. Spread the mixture thickly over the salmon, pressing to adhere.

3 Transfer to the oven and bake on the center rack until the salmon is flaky at the edges but not quite cooked through, 10 to 15 minutes.

4 Remove the pan from the oven and set the oven to broil. Slide the pan under the broiler and broil until the panko topping is crisp and golden and the salmon is opaque and flaky throughout, about 1 minute.

5 Serve hot.

HOW TO? REMOVE PIN BONES FROM FISH

How pesky are pin bones? There's nothing like a tiny pin bone to turn a succulent bite of fish into a choking hazard—*no bueno*. To remove pin bones from your fillets before cooking, place the fish skin-side down on a flat surface, and run your fingers over it to feel for the small, prickly line of bones (it's usually found toward the thicker, middle part of the fillet). Use a pair of needle-nose pliers or some (clean!) tweezers to grab the tips of the long, delicate bones and pull gently up and out. Feel your way all along the fillet to catch each last pin bone, removing them as you go.

COCONUT CURRY
SHRIMP WITH RICE

⌐ SERVES 4 TO 6 ⌐

COCONUT CURRY ON THE QUICK! AND PULLED from the oven, no less. Red curry paste, which you can find in the Asian foods section of most grocery stores, anchors the quickly whisked coconut curry sauce, which is simply poured over the shrimp and a bunch of frozen rice in a sturdy baking dish. After a brief jaunt in the oven, everyone will get to know each other and then we'll spoon this saucy, flavorful delight into bowls for all.

2 tablespoons red curry paste

2 teaspoons curry powder

1 (14-ounce) can coconut milk

2 tablespoons packed light brown sugar

1 tablespoon rice vinegar

1 tablespoon less-sodium soy sauce

½ teaspoon crushed red pepper

1 teaspoon kosher salt

1½ pounds medium shrimp, peeled and deveined

1 shallot, chopped

1 red or orange bell pepper, chopped

4 cups frozen rice

2 tablespoons chopped or chiffonade-cut fresh Thai basil (see tip, page 83)

2 tablespoons chopped scallion, white and light green parts only

½ lime

1 Preheat the oven to 375°F, with a rack in the center position.

2 In a large bowl, whisk together the red curry paste, curry powder, and coconut milk, adding the coconut milk slowly to prevent lumps. Whisk in the brown sugar, rice vinegar, soy sauce, crushed red pepper, and salt. Add the shrimp, shallot, and bell pepper and toss to coat.

3 Arrange the frozen rice around the sides of a 9 × 13-inch baking dish, leaving the center bare. Pour the shrimp and sauce into the center of the dish.

4 Cover the dish with foil, transfer to the oven, and bake for 30 minutes. Uncover the dish and bake until the shrimp are pink and opaque and the rice is moist and tender, 5 to 10 minutes longer.

5 Remove from the oven, toss the basil and scallion on top of the shrimp, and squeeze the fresh lime over it all. Serve hot.

MUSSELS
WITH
WHITE WINE, GARLIC & CHORIZO

⊷ SERVES 4 ⊶

SWEET AND BRINY MUSSELS ARE A DELIGHT TO cook at home in a big Dutch oven (with plenty of garlic and chorizo), although I'm mostly in it for the garlic toast and divinely flavored broth, if we're being honest. As my favorite culinary school instructor (a happily round Frenchman with impeccably white aprons) used to say: "Mussel juice changes everything!" And it's true. Is there anything better than dunking hearty bread in that sea-scented, wine-infused, lightly creamy broth? If you'd rather leave the pan on the stovetop to steam the mussels instead of transferring it to the oven, check them for doneness around 3 to 4 minutes.

2 tablespoons unsalted butter

2 tablespoons extra virgin olive oil

1 medium yellow onion, chopped

Kosher salt

4 cloves garlic, 3 minced and 1 peeled but whole

½ pound fresh chorizo, casings removed

1 cup white wine

1½ cups chicken broth

½ baguette, sliced in half crosswise, then again horizontally (to form 4 long pieces)

2½ pounds mussels, scrubbed and debearded

½ cup heavy cream

¼ cup chopped fresh flat-leaf parsley

1 Preheat the oven to 400°F, with a rack in the lower position.

2 Melt the butter in the olive oil in a large (7- to 8-quart) Dutch oven over medium-high heat. Add the onion with a pinch of salt and sauté until just soft, about 5 minutes. Add the minced garlic and chorizo, breaking it up as you stir it in, and cook until the meat is cooked through, 5 to 10 minutes.

3 Add the wine and deglaze the pan, scraping up the browned bits from the bottom, and bring to a boil. Add the broth and bring to a simmer.

4 While you wait for the pot to simmer, place the bread slices in the hot oven, directly on the rack, to toast.

5 When the broth is simmering, add the mussels to the pot and cover tightly. Transfer the pot to the oven and let the mussels steam until they open, about 7 minutes. Remove the pan from the oven, discard any mussels that haven't opened, and gently stir in the cream.

6 When the toast is golden, about 7 minutes, remove it from the oven and rub the whole garlic clove over the cut sides.

7 Sprinkle the parsley over the mussels and serve them immediately, with garlicky toast alongside for dipping.

NEW ENGLAND CLAM CHOWDER

SERVES 6 TO 8

1 tablespoon unsalted butter

¼ pound pancetta or slab bacon, diced

1 large leek, white and light green parts only, sliced into half-moons and cleaned well (see tip, page 137)

5 stalks celery, chopped

2 tablespoons all-purpose flour

2 (10-ounce) cans clams in juice, drained, juice reserved

3 Yukon Gold potatoes, cubed (about 2 cups)

2 cups seafood stock or vegetable broth

1 bay leaf

2 cups half-and-half

Kosher salt and ground black pepper

2 tablespoons chopped fresh flat-leaf parsley

2 tablespoons chopped fresh dill

¼ cup fresh lemon juice

Oyster crackers, for serving

MY GRANDPARENTS ARNIE AND LYNN LOVED each other fiercely and were married for sixty-two years, although they didn't always see eye to eye. For example, Gramma rooted for the Brooklyn Dodgers (back when they still existed) and PopPop loved the Yankees. Gramma was a flaming liberal, and PopPop often voted Republican. When we'd head to the docks near their house in Montauk, Gramma preferred tomato-based Manhattan clam chowder, and PopPop? He was a creamy New England kind of guy (although they both would have pronounced it "chowdah" and washed it down with a glass of vodka on the rocks). This recipe for rich, creamy "chowdah" is an homage to PopPop, who might have disapproved of my professional baseball allegiances, but always let me steal a few of his oyster crackers on chowder night.

1   Melt the butter in a medium (5- to 6-quart) Dutch oven over medium-high heat. Add the diced pancetta and cook until crisp. Add the leek and celery and cook until just soft, about 5 minutes.

2   Stir in the flour and cook for a minute, then stir in the reserved clam juice. Add the potatoes, stock, and bay leaf and bring the soup to a simmer. Reduce the heat to medium and simmer gently until the potatoes are tender, 20 to 30 minutes.

3   Stir in the clams, half-and-half, and a pinch each of salt and pepper. Continue cooking at a slow simmer until everything is nice and hot, about 10 minutes. Discard the bay leaf and stir in the parsley, dill, and lemon juice. Taste the soup and adjust the seasoning.

4   Serve hot, with oyster crackers alongside.

MEDITERRANEAN FISH STEW

SERVES 4

HERE'S A CLASSIC FISHERMAN'S STEW MADE easy! It's a humbly indulgent sort of dish, rich with fennel, potatoes, and flaky white fish. I call for anchovy paste to bump up the salty fish flavor—it might sound weird to you, but don't skip it! The briny, umami-ish paste really brings the flavor to the next level. If you can't find anchovy paste, just mash up 4 or 5 anchovy fillets instead. I like to serve this stew with plenty of garlic-rubbed toast, or a simple loaf of bread.

2 tablespoons extra virgin olive oil

1 yellow onion, chopped

2 large carrots, chopped

1 large bulb fennel, cored and thinly sliced

4 cloves garlic, minced

1 tablespoon anchovy paste

1 teaspoon dried oregano

1 (28-ounce) can diced tomatoes

4 cups water or chicken broth

1 pound small new potatoes, quartered

1 bay leaf

½ teaspoon fresh thyme leaves

Kosher salt and ground black pepper

1½ pounds firm white-fleshed fish (such as halibut, tilapia, or cod), cut into 2-inch pieces

¼ cup chopped fresh flat-leaf parsley

1 Heat the olive oil in a medium (5- to 6-quart) Dutch oven over medium-high heat. When the oil is shimmering, add the onion, carrots, and fennel and sauté until softened, about 10 minutes. Add the garlic, anchovy paste, and oregano and cook for 2 minutes more, stirring well to incorporate.

2 Add the tomatoes, water, potatoes, bay leaf, thyme, 1 teaspoon salt, and ½ teaspoon pepper. Bring the stew to a simmer, then reduce the heat to medium-low, partially cover, and simmer until the potatoes are tender, about 20 minutes.

3 Add the fish pieces to the pot and cook until the fish is opaque and flaky, 5 to 10 minutes. Taste the stew and adjust the seasoning, as you like. Discard the bay leaf.

4 Serve the stew hot, with the parsley scattered on top.

HERBY COD & ORZO WITH GREMOLATA

SERVES 4

LET'S COOK COD FILLETS AND ORZO TOGETHER in one pot, okay? We can invite some zucchini and onion and this cool new kid called "gremolata" (he sounds intimidating, but the only thing to him is garlic, lemon zest, herbs, and pistachios) and it'll be like a one pan party!—with tender pasta, flaky fish, and a crunchy, zingy topping. So what do you think? My place, say around seven? Great! See you there.

2 tablespoons unsalted butter

1 small onion, cut into ½-inch-thick slices

1 small zucchini, cut into ½-inch cubes

Kosher salt and ground black pepper

1 cup orzo

2 cups chicken or vegetable broth

4 (5-ounce) skinless cod fillets, pin bones removed (see tip, page 168)

1 tablespoon grated lemon zest

1 clove garlic, minced

¼ cup roughly chopped pistachios

2 tablespoons chopped fresh chives

1 teaspoon chopped fresh tarragon

1 Preheat the oven to 350°F, with a rack in the center position.

2 Melt the butter in a medium (5- to 6-quart) Dutch oven over medium-high heat. Add the onion, zucchini, ½ teaspoon salt, and a pinch of pepper and sauté until just softened, about 5 minutes.

3 Add the orzo and stir to coat with the oils from the pot. Stir in the broth and add the cod fillets. Transfer the pot to the oven and bake, covered, until the fish is opaque and flaky and the orzo is tender, about 20 minutes.

4 While the dish bakes, make the gremolata: Stir together the lemon zest, garlic, pistachios, chives, and tarragon in a small bowl.

5 Serve the fish fillets hot, scattered with the lemon-pistachio gremolata.

CHAPTER SIX

MEAT

Slow-Roasted BBQ Pulled Pork
Sandwiches 181

Weeknight Jambalaya 191

Lamb Meatballs with Spinach & Orzo 198

Gramma's Brisket with Carrots & Onions 202

Beef & Bean Chili with Warm Nacho Chips 204

Hearty Lentil Soup with Lardons 208

Spicy Sausage & Tortellini Soup 209

Spicy Miso Ramen with Ground Pork 211

Shepherd's Pot Pie 212

Sweet & Salty Pork Chops with Snow
Peas 183

Maple-Roasted Pork Tenderloin with Sweet
Potato Fries 186

Pork & Pineapple Pizza 189

Rosemary-Roasted Lamb Rib Chops &
New Potatoes 193

Broiled Beef & Broccoli 201

Sausages with Charred Onions & Tzatziki 203

BLT Baked Potatoes 207

Chickpea & Andouille Skillet 184

Broiled Burgers with Roasted Onions 187

Pan-Roasted Pork Chops with Butternut
Squash, Tomatoes & Sage 194

Seared Steak with Balsamic Burst
Tomatoes 197

SLOW-ROASTED BBQ PULLED PORK SANDWICHES

SLOW-ROASTED PULLED PORK TAKES TIME, yes, but never fear—after a quick dry rub and a sear on the stovetop, it only takes a few hours of letting-the-meat-do-its-thing-in-the-oven-while-you-catch-up-on-Netflix to be good and ready for dinner. I like to keep things simple by using store-bought barbecue sauce and tossing together a quick cabbage slaw to bring much needed freshness and crunch to this sweet, smoky, meltingly tender pork sandwich.

1½ teaspoons kosher salt

1½ teaspoons ground black pepper

1½ teaspoons sweet or smoked paprika

2 teaspoons ground cumin

1 tablespoon packed dark brown sugar

4 to 6 pounds boneless pork shoulder or butt

2 tablespoons vegetable oil

1 large yellow onion, roughly chopped

4 cloves garlic, smashed and peeled

1½ cups amber beer

1 cup barbecue sauce (I like Stubb's or Sweet Baby Ray's)

2 cups shredded red cabbage

2 scallions, white and light green parts only, chopped

¼ cup apple cider vinegar

¼ cup extra virgin olive oil

6 to 8 soft burger buns

1 Preheat the oven to 325°F.

2 In a small bowl, whisk together the salt, pepper, paprika, cumin, and brown sugar. Trim the pork of any large chunks of fat, then cut the meat into several fist-size chunks. Sprinkle the spice mixture over the pork and rub it evenly to coat.

3 Heat the vegetable oil in a large (7- to 8-quart) Dutch oven over medium-high heat. When the oil is shimmering, add the pork pieces and sear, turning, until browned on all sides, about 10 minutes. Add the onion and garlic and pour the beer over everything (the liquid should come about three-fourths of the way up the pork, not submerge it completely).

4 Bring to a simmer, then cover the pot and transfer to the oven. Roast the pork for 2 hours, then begin to check it every half hour or so for doneness. The pork is done when it starts to break apart as you nudge it with a fork.

RECIPE CONTINUES

5 Transfer the pork to a large bowl, reserving the cooking liquid in the pan. When it's cool enough to handle, shred the pork into pieces with your fingers or two forks. (You can shred the soft onion in with the meat, if you like.)

6 Moisten the shredded pork with ½ cup or so of the reserved cooking liquid and stir in the barbecue sauce.

7 In a separate bowl, stir together the cabbage, scallions, cider vinegar, olive oil, and salt and pepper to taste.

8 Pile the pulled pork onto the soft burger buns and top with the cabbage slaw. Serve immediately.

9 Extra pulled pork will keep in an airtight container in the refrigerator for up to 1 week or in the freezer for up to 3 months.

SWEET & SALTY
PORK
CHOPS
WITH
SNOW PEAS

SERVES 4 TO 6

THIN-CUT BONELESS PORK CHOPS COOK UP IN no time on a sheet pan under the broiler, so after a brief sweet-and-sour bath, they're ready to go in minutes! Charred snow peas make a nice, crisp accompaniment and soak up any extra glazey marinade. I like to serve this one with rice alongside.

1 tablespoon grated fresh ginger

½ cup less-sodium soy sauce

2 tablespoons toasted sesame oil

½ cup peach jam

¼ cup apple cider vinegar

2 cloves garlic, minced

½ teaspoon crushed red pepper

2 tablespoons fresh lime juice

6 thin-cut boneless pork chops

5 cups snow peas

1 Preheat the oven to 400°F, with one rack in the center position and another 4 inches from the broiler. Line a sheet pan with foil or mist with cooking spray.

2 In a medium bowl, whisk together the ginger, soy sauce, sesame oil, peach jam, vinegar, garlic, crushed red pepper, and lime juice. Measure out ½ cup of the marinade and set aside. Pour the rest over the pork chops to marinate (I like to do this in a zip-top bag).

3 Toss the snow peas with the reserved marinade on the prepared sheet pan and spread out in an even layer. Transfer to the oven and roast on the center rack for 10 minutes.

4 Remove the pan from the oven and set the oven to broil. Place a well-greased wire rack over the snow peas. Place the chops on the rack, slide under the broiler, and broil until a thermometer inserted into the center of a pork chop reads 140° to 145°F and the snow peas are nicely charred, 4 to 5 minutes, flipping the chops halfway through cooking.

5 Serve hot.

CHICKPEA & ANDOUILLE SKILLET

THIS RUSTIC, NOURISHING SKILLET FEELS LIKE peasant food—in the best way possible, I mean. It feels like what we might eat on the regular if we lived somewhere exotic, like Spain or Tuscany. We'd walk to the local market and pick up some fat carrots, local goat cheese, and freshly smoked sausages (wearing all white linen, probably, because we are more chic in Europe) and then we'd head back to our sunlit flat, grab our centuries-old, well-seasoned cast iron pan, and whip up this hearty dish. I'd scatter the chickpeas artfully around the pan, you'd pour the wine, we'd feast like kings, and then take a nap on the patio.

2 tablespoons extra virgin olive oil

½ red onion, finely chopped

1 large carrot, finely chopped

3 stalks celery, finely chopped

1 clove garlic, finely chopped

¼ teaspoon kosher salt

¼ teaspoon ground black pepper

6 andouille sausages, sliced on an angle into ½-inch-thick slices

1 (15-ounce) can chickpeas, drained and rinsed

2 oil-packed sun-dried tomatoes, chopped

½ cup chicken broth

1 (4-ounce) log herbed goat cheese, crumbled

¼ cup chopped fresh flat-leaf parsley

1 Preheat the oven to 350°F, with a rack in the center position.

2 Heat the oil in a 10-inch cast iron skillet over medium-high heat. When the oil is shimmering, add the onion, carrot, and celery and cook until soft and beginning to brown, about 7 minutes. Add the garlic, salt, and pepper and cook for 1 minute. Add the sausages, chickpeas, and sun-dried tomatoes and sauté until the sausages start to brown, about 5 minutes.

3 Add the broth and scrape up the browned bits from the bottom of the pan. Cook for about 2 minutes to evaporate most of the liquid.

4 Scatter the goat cheese over the skillet and transfer it to the oven. Bake until the cheese is melty and the skillet is fragrant and brown, about 10 minutes.

5 Serve hot, topped with the parsley.

METHOD MADNESS

If you'd like to add eggs to this dish to make it extra hearty or to serve it for brunch, crack a few over the skillet just before adding the goat cheese (see tip, page 24), and bake in the oven until just set.

MAPLE-ROASTED
PORK TENDERLOIN
WITH
SWEET POTATO FRIES

⌐ **SERVES 4 TO 6** ⌐

BUT SERIOUSLY, DID YOU SAY FRIES? THESE crisp, oven-baked fries are totally addicting, and the best part is that they cook up underneath a mustardy, mapley, herby pork tenderloin! It's a simple, fun take on a classic pairing that'll have you reaching into the depths of your purse for that handy bottle of ketchup that you definitely don't keep in there for French-fry-mergencies.

3 tablespoons Dijon mustard

3 tablespoons pure maple syrup

1 tablespoon extra virgin olive oil

½ teaspoon ground sage

½ teaspoon dried thyme

Kosher salt and ground black pepper

2 pork tenderloins (about 1 pound each)

2 pounds sweet potatoes (about 2½ potatoes), cut lengthwise into ½-inch wedges

2 tablespoons canola oil

1 Preheat the oven to 450°F, with a rack in the center position. Line a sheet pan with foil or mist with cooking spray.

2 In a medium bowl, whisk together the mustard, maple syrup, olive oil, sage, thyme, ½ teaspoon salt, and ¼ teaspoon pepper until smooth. Add the pork and turn to coat completely. Set aside.

3 Toss the sweet potato wedges with the canola oil and ½ teaspoon each salt and pepper on the prepared sheet pan. Arrange the potatoes in an even layer, transfer to the oven, and roast for about 15 minutes, until just starting to brown. Remove from the oven and gently toss the fries on the pan.

4 Coat a wire rack with cooking spray and set it over the sweet potatoes in the pan. Place the pork tenderloins on top, spacing them apart evenly. Return the pan to the oven and roast, flipping the tenderloins halfway through cooking, until the fries are charred and crisp and a thermometer inserted into the thickest part of the pork registers 145°F, about 30 minutes more.

5 Allow the tenderloins to rest for 10 minutes before thinly slicing and serving warm, with the fries alongside.

BROILED **BURGERS** WITH ROASTED ONIONS

BROILING BURGERS IN A CAST IRON SKILLET keeps them moist and juicy, and piling them high with soft roasted onions (from that same cast iron skillet, of course) and cheddar cheese? Pro move. Extra points for soft buns and lots of pickles.

1½ small yellow onions, sliced into ¼-inch-thick half-moons

2 tablespoons extra virgin olive oil

1 tablespoon balsamic vinegar

Kosher salt and ground black pepper

1 pound ground beef

2 tablespoons Worcestershire sauce

2 tablespoons garlic powder

4 slices sharp cheddar cheese

4 hamburger buns

Ketchup, pickles, lettuce, and sliced tomatoes, for serving

1 Preheat the oven to 375°F, with one rack in the center position and another about 4 inches from the broiler.

2 Toss the onions in a 10-inch cast iron skillet with the olive oil, balsamic, and a pinch each of salt and pepper. Transfer the pan to the center rack of the oven and roast the onions until soft and beginning to brown, 20 to 25 minutes.

3 While the onions roast, make the burgers: In a large bowl, use your hands to gently mix together the beef, Worcestershire, garlic powder, ¼ teaspoon salt, and ¼ teaspoon pepper. Working gently to avoid tough burgers (resist the urge to squeeze and pack tightly), form the mixture into 4 patties, each about 1½ inches thick.

4 Remove the pan from the oven and set the oven to broil. Place the burger patties on top of the softened onions in the skillet, then slide the pan under the broiler. Broil the burgers and onions for 6 to 8 minutes for medium-rare, flipping the burgers halfway through. (If you want your burgers either more or less cooked, adjust the cooking time accordingly.)

5 Pull the pan out of the oven, top each burger with a slice of cheese, and return to the broiler for 1 minute longer to melt the cheese. While the cheese melts, place the buns cut-side down on the center rack to warm.

6 Serve the burgers hot from the oven, piled on warm buns with heaps of soft, charred onions and plenty of fixings.

PORK & PINEAPPLE PIZZA

○ SERVES 4 TO 6 ○

MY DAD THINKS PINEAPPLE BELONGS ON *everything,* pizza in particular, so this one is for him. I will say that it absolutely works here—the sweet fruit cutting nicely through the salty meat, zesty green chiles, and ample cheese. Making pizza dough from scratch is the kind of thing that's intimidating until you do it once, at which point you realize OF COURSE you can make your own pizza dough, and make it well, but if you're pressed for time or just not into the idea, feel free to use a store-bought ball.

2¾ cups bread flour, plus more for working the dough

1 cup whole wheat pastry flour

2½ teaspoons rapid-rise yeast

¾ teaspoon kosher salt

¾ teaspoon sugar

1½ cups plus 2 tablespoons warm water

3 tablespoons extra virgin olive oil

1 cup shredded low-moisture mozzarella cheese (4 ounces)

4 slices Black Forest ham (about 3 ounces), cut into strips

8 pineapple rings (fresh or canned)

2 tablespoons canned diced green chiles

1 cup grated sharp cheddar cheese (4 ounces)

1 teaspoon chopped fresh thyme leaves

½ teaspoon dried oregano

1 In a large bowl, whisk together the flours, yeast, salt, and sugar. Add the warm water and mix with a wooden spoon or rubber spatula to form a shaggy but cohesive dough. If mixing becomes difficult, just use your hands to work the dough instead. Cover the bowl with plastic wrap and then with a clean kitchen towel. Set it aside at room temperature to rise until the dough has doubled in size, about 1 hour.

2 Meanwhile, preheat the oven to 500°F, with a rack in the upper third. Drizzle 2 tablespoons of the olive oil onto a sheet pan, then tilt the pan around to evenly distribute the oil—you want the pan liberally greased.

3 When the dough has risen, turn it out onto a lightly floured work surface. Use a sharp, floured knife to divide it evenly in half. Wrap one portion tightly in plastic wrap, place it in a zip-top bag, and store it in the freezer for later use. (Thaw it overnight in the fridge, then let it come to room temperature before using.)

RECIPE CONTINUES

4 Place the portion of dough you're using on the oiled sheet pan. Flour your hands and press and stretch the dough into the pan, until it nearly reaches the edges. (If it rips, just pinch it back together.) If the dough starts to spring back and shrink while you're pressing it out, allow it to rest for 5 minutes, then resume pressing. You should end up with a flat, roughly ½-inch-thick rectangle of dough.

5 Brush the dough all the way to the edges with the remaining 1 tablespoon olive oil. Sprinkle the mozzarella on top, leaving about a ½-inch border around the edges for the crust. Layer the ham, pineapple, and green chiles over the mozzarella, then top with the cheddar, thyme, and oregano.

6 Transfer the pizza to the oven and bake until the crust is deeply brown and the cheese is browned and bubbling, 18 to 20 minutes.

7 Let the pizza cool slightly before slicing it into squares or rectangles. Serve hot.

WEEKNIGHT JAMBALAYA

◦ SERVES 4 TO 6 ◦

JAMBALAYA, A CLASSIC CREOLE DISH FROM New Orleans, traditionally involves chicken, shrimp, rice, andouille sausage, and plenty of time on the stovetop to build and layer flavor. But I wanted a quicker weeknight version that wouldn't force me to visit every aisle in the supermarket and spend an hour standing over a bubbling pot. This version stays true to the original in certain ways (we start with a sofrito of onion, celery, and bell pepper, for example), but nixes a few ingredients (so long, chicken! Sausage and shrimp will do) and cooks inside the oven, as our favorite hassle-free, one pan method is wont to do. So we can spend more time letting *les bons temps rouler*! Which is the whole point, isn't it?

2 tablespoons extra virgin olive oil

1 large yellow onion, chopped (about 4 cups)

1 red bell pepper, chopped (about 2 cups)

4 stalks celery, chopped (about 2 cups), tops and leaves reserved and roughly chopped

14 ounces smoked sausage, cut into ½-inch-thick slices

2 cloves garlic, minced

2 teaspoons sweet paprika

¼ teaspoon cayenne pepper

1 teaspoon dried oregano

2 teaspoons kosher salt

½ teaspoon ground black pepper

1½ cups white rice

1 (14.5-ounce) can diced tomatoes

2 cups low sodium chicken broth

1 bay leaf

1 pound peeled and deveined shrimp (26/30 count), tails removed

1   Preheat the oven to 375°F, with a rack in the center position.

2   Heat the olive oil in a medium (5- to 6-quart) Dutch oven over medium-high heat. When the oil is shimmering, add the onion, bell pepper, and celery stalks and cook until beginning to soften, about 5 minutes. Stir in the sausage, garlic, paprika, cayenne, oregano, salt, and black pepper and cook for another 5 minutes. Add the rice, stirring to coat with oil, then add the tomatoes, broth, and bay leaf. Bring the jambalaya to a boil, cover the pot, and transfer it to the oven.

3   Bake until the rice is just underdone, about 20 minutes. Remove from the oven, stir in the shrimp, return the pot to the oven, and bake until the rice is tender and the shrimp are pink and opaque, 5 to 10 minutes longer. Discard the bay leaf.

4   Serve hot, garnished with the chopped celery tops and leaves.

ROSEMARY-ROASTED
LAMB RIB CHOPS & NEW POTATOES

SERVES 4 TO 6

THIS RECIPE IS FOR WHEN YOU WANT TO impress your guests with very minimal actual effort. One look at this beautiful pan and everyone will "ooh!" and "aah!" and no one has to know how easy it was to roast some potatoes on a sheet pan, then rub little lamb chops with brown sugar and rosemary and shove the lot under the broiler. Although the classic red creamers called for work very nicely, small multicolored potatoes make the dish extra pretty.

2½ to 3 pounds red creamer potatoes, quartered (6 to 8 cups)

¼ cup plus 2 tablespoons extra virgin olive oil

¾ teaspoon kosher salt

¼ cup packed light brown sugar

1 tablespoon chopped fresh rosemary

3 cloves garlic, finely diced

¼ teaspoon dried thyme

¼ teaspoon ground black pepper

8 to 12 lamb rib chops (1 to 1½ pounds), separated into individual chops

1   Preheat the oven to 375°F, with one rack in the center position and another 5 inches from the broiler. Line a sheet pan with foil or mist with cooking spray.

2   Toss the potatoes, 2 tablespoons of the olive oil, and ¼ teaspoon of the salt together on the prepared sheet pan. Spread out in an even layer and bake until the potatoes are tender and their edges are crisp, 30 to 35 minutes.

3   While the potatoes roast, in a small bowl, mix together the brown sugar, rosemary, garlic, thyme, remaining ¼ cup olive oil, ½ teaspoon salt, and the black pepper. Rub the mixture thickly over the chops. Coat a wire rack with cooking spray and place the chops in an even layer on the rack.

4   When the potatoes are tender, remove the pan from the oven and set the oven to broil. Place the rack with the lamb over the potatoes.

5   Return to the oven and broil until the lamb is charred on the outside, tender within, and a thermometer inserted into the thickest part reads 130°F for medium-rare, about 3 minutes, flipping the chops halfway.

6   Serve hot.

PAN-ROASTED PORK CHOPS

WITH BUTTERNUT SQUASH, TOMATOES & SAGE

— SERVES 2 —

BUTTERNUT SQUASH, SHALLOT, AND SAGE ARE old friends, and play beautifully with meaty pork chops and sweet, end-of-season cherry tomatoes in this bright, cozy, autumn-flavored skillet. The vibrant colors practically jump out of the pan, and the whole thing is almost too pretty to eat! . . . Almost.

1½ cups peeled and cubed butternut squash (½-inch cubes)

1 tablespoon extra virgin olive oil, plus more if needed

1 small shallot, chopped

7 fresh sage leaves

Kosher salt and ground black pepper

2 bone-in pork chops (about 8 ounces each)

½ cup cherry tomatoes

1 Preheat the oven to 400°F, with a rack in the center position.

2 Toss the squash with the olive oil, shallot, sage leaves, and a pinch each of salt and pepper in a 10-inch cast iron skillet. Transfer to the oven and roast until the squash is just beginning to brown, 15 to 20 minutes.

3 Carefully remove the pan from the oven and place it on the stovetop over medium-high heat. Push the squash to the sides of the pan and place the pork chops in the center (add a splash more olive oil if the pan seems dry). Sprinkle the chops with a pinch each of salt and pepper and sear for 3 minutes.

4 Flip the chops and add the tomatoes. Return the pan to the oven and roast until the squash is tender, the tomatoes have burst, and a thermometer inserted into the thickest part of the chops reads 150°F, 8 to 12 minutes.

5 Serve hot.

SEARED STEAK

WITH

BALSAMIC BURST TOMATOES

SERVES 2

IF YOU'RE LOOKING FOR A FOOLPROOF WAY to cook steak, this is me waving my arms wildly at you because the recipe is here! A quick sear in a hot cast iron skillet gives our steak the perfect crust, and finishing it off in the oven with some balsamic-tossed cherry tomatoes ensures an evenly pink center and a tangy, tomatoey glaze. I like using New York strip steaks, which are sometimes called Kansas City strip or top sirloin (not to be confused with sirloin steak), because they've got enough marbling to give great flavor, but no large pockets of fat to deal with. You could get fancy and use cuts of filet mignon, but you'll want to check for doneness after just a few minutes in the oven, as they're much leaner and tend to dry out more quickly.

1 tablespoon vegetable oil
1 (1-pound) boneless New York Strip steak
Kosher salt and ground black pepper
10 ounces (about 1½ cups) cherry tomatoes
3 tablespoons balsamic vinegar

1 Preheat the oven to 400°F, with a rack in the center position.

2 Heat the vegetable oil in a 10-inch cast iron skillet over high heat. Blot the steak dry with a paper towel, then season it on both sides with a generous pinch of salt and pepper. When the oil is shimmering, add the steak and sear until a crust forms, about 2 minutes per side.

3 While the steak sears, in a medium bowl, toss the tomatoes with balsamic vinegar and a pinch each of salt and pepper.

4 Add the tomatoes to the hot pan, then transfer the pan to the oven. Roast until a thermometer inserted into the thickest part of the steak reads 130°F for medium-rare, about 15 minutes. (Adjust the cooking time a bit if you prefer more or less done steak.)

5 Let the steak rest on a cutting board for 10 minutes before slicing it thinly against the grain. Serve the meat warm, with the burst tomatoes alongside.

LAMB MEATBALLS
WITH
SPINACH & ORZO

〜 SERVES 4 TO 6 〜

IT TOOK ME A WHILE TO APPRECIATE THE RICH, almost grassy flavor of lamb, but cooking with ground lamb is a treat. Don't be intimidated! It pretty much behaves just like beef. These meatballs have a flavor both deep and bright, but also with plenty of zip from fresh lemon zest and crumbled feta. Our trusty Dutch oven lets us cook both the meatballs and the orzo at once, and the resulting dish is creamy, meaty, and richly satisfying.

1½ pounds ground lamb

9 ounces frozen spinach, thawed and squeezed dry

½ medium red onion, finely chopped (about 1 cup)

½ cup feta cheese, plus more for topping

1 egg, beaten

¼ cup Italian-style bread crumbs

2 cloves garlic, very finely chopped

1 teaspoon grated lemon zest

3 tablespoons extra virgin olive oil

1 teaspoon kosher salt

½ teaspoon ground black pepper

1½ cups orzo

3 cups low-sodium chicken broth

2 tablespoons chopped fresh mint

1 Preheat the oven to 350°F, with a rack in the center position.

2 In a large bowl, gently combine the lamb, spinach, onion, feta cheese, egg, bread crumbs, garlic, lemon zest, 1 tablespoon of the olive oil, the salt, and pepper until well mixed. Form the mixture into 1½-inch meatballs, being careful not to squeeze the mixture too vigorously (working gently ensures tender meatballs).

3 Heat the remaining 2 tablespoons olive oil in a medium (5- to 6-quart) Dutch oven over medium-high heat. When the oil is shimmering, add the meatballs and cook, turning, until browned all over, about 10 minutes. Remove and set aside on a plate to rest.

4 Add the orzo to the Dutch oven and stir to coat with the oils in the pan. Stir in the broth, then return the meatballs to the pan.

5 Cover the pot and bake until the orzo has absorbed most of the liquid and a thermometer inserted into the largest meatball reads 160°F, about 30 minutes. Uncover and continue baking until the orzo is completely tender, about 10 minutes. If it doesn't look like the liquid is totally absorbed but the orzo is well done, give the pot a gentle stir to incorporate the liquid.

6 Serve warm, topped with some feta and the mint.

FUN HACK!
MEATBALL SHORTCUT

I've included instructions to brown the meatballs first, before adding the orzo, because I like the dark color and caramelized flavor it imparts, but if you're short on time (or patience), you can definitely skip this step—just add the raw meatballs to the orzo immediately after adding the chicken broth, then proceed with the recipe as written.

BROILED
BEEF
&
BROCCOLI

— SERVES 4 TO 6 —

THIS TWIST ON STIR-FRY HAS THE DEEP, toasty flavor of classic beef and broccoli, but loses the stir-fry part. Why stand over a hot wok wrangling oil splatters when you don't have to? After a short marinade, flank steak cooks in mere minutes under the broiler, getting a nice brown crust and a sweet, savory glaze. The broccoli florets and meaty shiitake mushrooms cook right alongside, getting perfectly charred and ready for a tumble over a bowl of rice, which is a nice accompaniment, if you like.

⅓ cup less-sodium soy sauce

¼ cup toasted sesame oil

1 tablespoon packed light brown sugar

3 cloves garlic, minced

1 (2-inch) piece fresh ginger, grated

2½ pounds flank steak

4 cups broccoli florets

2 cups shiitake mushrooms, halved

2 tablespoons extra virgin olive oil

1 Preheat the oven to 375°F, with one rack in the center position and another 4 inches from the broiler. Line a sheet pan with foil or mist with cooking spray.

2 In a medium bowl, whisk together the soy sauce, sesame oil, brown sugar, garlic, and ginger. Measure out ¼ cup of the marinade and set aside. Add the steak to the remainder, turning to coat. Let sit while you prepare the rest of the dish.

3 Toss the broccoli florets and shiitake mushrooms on the prepared pan with the olive oil and reserved marinade. Spread everything out in an even layer on the pan, transfer to the oven, and roast on the center rack until just tender, about 10 minutes. Remove the pan from the oven and set the oven to broil.

4 Push the broccoli and mushrooms to the edges of the pan and place the steak in the center, drizzling over any remaining marinade. Slide the pan under the broiler and broil until the steak begins to char on the outside and a thermometer inserted into the thickest part of the meat registers 125°F for rare or 135°F for medium-rare, 3 to 5 minutes per side.

5 Remove the pan from the oven and let the steak rest, loosely covered with foil, for 10 minutes before thinly slicing against the grain. Serve warm, with the vegetables alongside.

GRAMMA'S
BRISKET
WITH
CARROTS
& ONIONS

> ⊸ SERVES 6 TO 8 ⊷

THIS IS CLASSIC JEWISH BRISKET, GRAMMA Marilyn–style, and if it's not pure love and comfort on a plate, then I don't know what is. It's best to start this dish a day or two before you want to serve it—one to marinate and two to let it cool, making the meat much easier to slice. Grams liked to serve it over buttery egg noodles, but it also goes well with some crusty bread for soaking up all of the rich sauce.

1 (4½- to 5-pound) beef brisket

4 cloves garlic, thinly sliced

1 tablespoon sweet paprika

1 tablespoon dried oregano

2 teaspoons mustard powder

1 teaspoon kosher salt

½ teaspoon ground black pepper

6 small onions, cut into ¼- to ½-inch-thick slices (about 8 cups)

5 medium carrots, peeled and cut into 2-inch chunks

1 (12-ounce) bottle chili sauce (I like Heinz)

3 cups red wine (I like to use a medium- to full-bodied variety, like Malbec, Petite Sirah, or Côtes du Rhône)

1 Using a sharp knife, make small, ½-inch-deep cuts all over the meat on both sides, and stuff the little cuts with the sliced garlic. Rub the paprika, oregano, mustard powder, salt, and pepper all over the meat, coating it generously. If you have time, place the brisket into a large zip-top bag and allow the meat to marinate in the refrigerator overnight.

2 Preheat the oven to 325°F.

3 Place a large (7- to 8-quart) Dutch oven over medium-high heat. When the pan is just smoking, add the brisket and sear until well browned, about 3 minutes per side. Remove the pan from the heat, cover the meat with the onions and carrots, and pour the chili sauce and wine on top.

4 Cover the pan, transfer to the oven, and bake until the meat is fork-tender, 2½ to 3 hours, flipping it halfway through. Remove the pan from the oven and allow it to cool slightly before storing it in the refrigerator, preferably overnight.

5 When you're ready to serve the brisket, preheat the oven to 325°F.

6 Remove the meat from the pot and slice it against the grain as thinly as possible. Return the slices to the pot, cover, transfer to the oven, and bake for 35 to 45 minutes to heat through.

7 Serve hot.

SAUSAGES
WITH
CHARRED ONIONS & TZATZIKI

SERVES 4

ON NIGHTS WHEN TIME IS TIGHT AND STOM-achs are rumbling, this modest, fuss-free pan of roasted sausages and onions hits the spot, and quick. Mixing up a simple tzatziki sauce—fresh and tangy with yogurt, cucumber, garlic, lemon juice, and parsley—is an easy step that really makes this dish shine.

2 large red onions, cut into ½-inch-thick slices

4 tablespoons extra virgin olive oil

½ teaspoon dried oregano

Kosher salt and ground black pepper

6 links sweet or hot Italian sausage (about 1½ pounds total)

2 cups plain Greek yogurt

1 cup finely chopped cucumber

2 tablespoons chopped fresh flat-leaf parsley

1 clove garlic, minced

1 tablespoon fresh lemon juice

1 tablespoon chopped fresh mint

1 Preheat the oven to 425°F, with a rack in the center position. Line a sheet pan with foil or mist with cooking spray.

2 Toss the onions with 3 tablespoons of the olive oil, the oregano, and ¼ teaspoon salt on the prepared sheet pan. Arrange the sausages evenly on and around the onions, and prick each sausage once or twice with a fork. Transfer to the oven and bake until the onions are soft and charred at the edges and the sausages are cooked through, about 30 minutes.

3 While the sausages cook, make the tzatziki sauce: In a medium bowl, mix together the yogurt, cucumber, parsley, garlic, lemon juice, remaining 1 tablespoon olive oil, and salt and pepper to taste.

4 Serve the sausages and onions hot, sprinkled with the mint and with the cool tzatziki sauce alongside.

BEEF & BEAN CHILI
WITH
WARM NACHO CHIPS

⟨ SERVES 6 TO 8 ⟩

WHAT'S BETTER THAN A POT OF PERFECTLY spiced chili? A pot of perfectly spiced chili *covered with nachos*, that's what. The rich flavors of the chili are built on the stovetop, then everything simmers in the oven to get cozy. And finally? The whole pot gets covered with warm, cheesy chips, because your happiness means a lot to me. Just be sure to serve with plenty of chili/nacho fixings—sour cream, scallions, and jalapeños are a good start.

METHOD MADNESS

You could make this chili entirely on the stovetop, but I like letting it simmer in the oven so I'm not tempted to check on it and stir every few minutes.

1 tablespoon extra virgin olive oil

3 pounds ground beef

2 tablespoons chili powder

2 teaspoons sweet or smoked paprika

2 teaspoons ground cumin

2 teaspoons kosher salt

1 small yellow onion, chopped

1 small red bell pepper, chopped

3 cloves garlic, finely chopped

2 teaspoons tomato paste

2 chipotles in adobo sauce, chopped (1 tablespoon adobo sauce reserved)

2 (28-ounce) cans diced tomatoes

1 (15-ounce) can kidney beans, drained and rinsed

1 (15-ounce) can black beans, drained and rinsed

1 (15-ounce) can cannellini beans, drained and rinsed

1 (14.5-ounce) can beef broth

4 to 5 cups tortilla chips

1½ cups shredded Mexican cheese blend (about 6 ounces)

Chili fixings, for serving

1   Preheat the oven to 400°F, with a rack in the center position.

2   Heat the oil in a medium (5- to 6-quart) Dutch oven over medium-high heat. When the oil is shimmering, add the beef and cook, stirring to break up the meat, until browned. Drain off any excess fat, if desired, and stir in the spices and salt. Add the onion, bell pepper, garlic, tomato paste, chipotle, and 1 tablespoon adobo sauce, stirring well to combine. Cook until the onion and pepper begin to soften, about 5 minutes. Add the tomatoes, beans, and broth and bring the chili to a simmer.

3   Bake until it begins to thicken, about 30 minutes. Remove the pot from the oven and place a thick layer of tortilla chips over the chili. Top generously with the shredded cheese. Return the pot to the oven and bake for 10 minutes to crisp the chips and melt the cheese.

4   Use a big spoon to break through the cheesy chips, and serve big bowls of chili and chips with plenty of your favorite fixings alongside.

BLT
BAKED
POTATOES

SERVES 4 TO 6

WELCOME, FRIENDS AND FAMILY, TO THE MAR-riage of two classic American favorites. We're gathered here today to witness the union of salty, crunchy BLT and Baked Potato, that big, buttery softie. This long-anticipated union will bring love and happiness (not to mention dinner) to many, so if anyone here knows of a reason these two tasty morsels should not be joined in arugula, please speak now, or forever hold your sheet pan peace.

8 to 10 slices bacon

4 to 6 large russet potatoes, scrubbed and pricked all over with a fork

2 cups cherry or grape tomatoes

2 tablespoons extra virgin olive oil

Kosher salt and ground black pepper

4 to 6 tablespoons unsalted butter

4 to 6 handfuls baby arugula

1 Preheat the oven to 400°F, with a rack in the center. Line a sheet pan with foil or mist with cooking spray.

2 Lay the bacon side by side on the sheet pan. Transfer to the oven and bake until it starts to crisp at the edges, about 15 minutes, then carefully flip the bacon and continue to cook until very crisp, another 10 minutes or so. Remove the pan from the oven and increase the oven temperature to 425°F.

3 Remove the bacon from the pan and set aside. Roll the potatoes in the bacon fat on the hot sheet pan, then space them evenly apart. Return the pan to the oven and bake the potatoes until the skins are crisp and the interiors are fork-tender, 45 minutes to 1 hour. Remove the pan from the oven, but keep the oven on.

4 Make a deep lengthwise slit in each potato. Carefully (they're hot!) push the ends of each potato together to expose some of the soft flesh.

5 In a medium bowl, toss the cherry tomatoes with the olive oil and a pinch each of salt and pepper. Scatter them on the pan around the potatoes. Place 1 tablespoon of butter on top of each potato. Add a pinch each of salt and pepper. Top each potato with a generous handful of baby arugula (it's okay if it falls off onto the pan).

6 Return the pan to the oven and bake until the tomatoes are warm and puckered and the arugula has wilted, about 5 minutes.

7 Meanwhile, crumble the bacon into bite-size pieces.

8 Serve the potatoes warm, topped with the roasted tomatoes and crumbled bacon.

HEARTY
LENTIL
SOUP
WITH
LARDONS

⊱ **SERVES 6 TO 8** ⊰

ON A COLD, WET WINTER EVENING (AND IT turns out there are quite a few of these in Seattle), all I want is a big bowlful of this warm and homey lentil soup. *Lardon* is just a fancy word for sliced, thick-cut bacon and, as you might imagine, it's the bacon that really takes this soup over the edge of fantastic. Using French green lentils helps, too, because they hold their shape well and impart a delicate, earthy flavor, but you could easily substitute regular brown lentils, if necessary.

10 ounces thick-cut bacon (about 8 slices), cut into ½-inch-thick lardons

2 medium onions, chopped (about 3 cups)

3 medium carrots, chopped (about 2 cups)

4 stalks celery, chopped (about 2 cups)

8 ounces cremini mushrooms, sliced (about 2 cups)

3 cloves garlic, finely chopped

1 tablespoon roughly chopped fresh thyme leaves

1 teaspoon kosher salt

1 teaspoon ground black pepper

2 cups French green lentils, rinsed

10 cups low-sodium chicken broth

1 Cook the bacon in a large (7- to 8-quart) Dutch oven over medium-high heat, stirring occasionally, until browned and crisp. Use tongs or a slotted spoon to remove the bacon from the pan and transfer to a plate lined with paper towels to drain.

2 Add the onions, carrots, celery, and mushrooms to the bacon fat in the pan and sauté until beginning to soften, about 7 minutes. Add the garlic, thyme, salt, and pepper, stirring to incorporate.

3 Stir in the lentils, add the broth, and bring the soup to a boil. Reduce the heat to medium-low, cover, and cook until the lentils are tender, about 40 minutes. Add the crisp lardons and stir to incorporate.

4 Taste the soup and add a bit more salt or pepper, if you like. Serve hot.

SPICY SAUSAGE & TORTELLINI SOUP

SERVES 6 TO 8

THIS WARMING, MEATY SOUP IS STOP-TO-take-a-deep-breath spicy, bright with fresh kale, and lush with cheesy pasta pockets. To make it in advance (and to be a weeknight hero), do everything except add the pasta, and store the soup in an airtight container in the fridge or freezer. Just before serving, bring the soup up to a simmer and add the tortellini.

1 tablespoon unsalted butter

1 tablespoon extra virgin olive oil

1 onion, finely chopped

1 bulb fennel, cored and finely chopped

4 cloves garlic, minced

1½ teaspoons chopped fresh thyme

½ teaspoon crushed red pepper

¾ pound smoked kielbasa, thinly sliced

6 cups low-sodium chicken broth

2 cups chopped fresh kale

1 (15-ounce) can cannellini beans, drained and rinsed

1½ cups grated Parmesan cheese (about 6 ounces), plus more for topping

1 (9-ounce) package fresh cheese tortellini (see tip, page 103)

1   Melt the butter in the olive oil in a medium (5- to 6-quart) Dutch oven over medium-high heat. Add the onion and fennel and sauté until soft and translucent, about 5 minutes. Add the garlic, thyme, and crushed red pepper and sauté for another 2 minutes, until fragrant. Add the kielbasa and cook until browned in spots.

2   Add the broth and bring the soup to a gentle boil. Add the kale and cannellini beans, then reduce the heat to medium-low and simmer until the kale is slightly wilted, about 5 minutes. Add the Parmesan, a little bit at a time, stirring to incorporate and melt into the soup.

3   Add the tortellini and simmer the soup until the pasta is just tender, but not overly soft (it should still be slightly firm to the bite), 2 to 5 minutes.

4   Serve immediately, with extra grated Parmesan on top.

SPICY MISO RAMEN WITH GROUND PORK

⊱ SERVES 4 TO 6 ⊰

MY HUSBAND AND I ARE CHEAP DATES—OUR favorite pick is the local ramen joint, where about once a week we can be found sitting across from each other, sipping beers and slurping noodles with abandon. Though we often think about branching out and ordering something *other* than the spicy miso ramen, we rarely ever do—because why mess with salty, spicy perfection? My homemade version swaps ground pork for the thick slabs of fatty pork that we get in the restaurant, and I think I like it even better. Plus, this way I can customize the toppings to my liking, which is usually an extra spoonful of corn, a good handful of fresh bean sprouts, and plenty of dried seaweed.

2 tablespoons toasted sesame oil

1 pound ground pork

2 tablespoons white miso paste

2 tablespoons sambal oelek

¼ cup low-sodium soy sauce

8 cups low-sodium chicken broth

1 cup frozen corn kernels

½ cup chopped scallions, white and light green parts only

3 packages ramen noodles

1 (8-ounce) can sliced bamboo shoots, drained

2 cups fresh bean sprouts

Dried seaweed squares (such as Trader Joe's Roasted Seaweed Snack squares)

1 Heat the sesame oil in a medium (5- to 6-quart) Dutch oven over medium-high heat. When the oil is shimmering, add the pork and cook, breaking it up with a wooden spoon or spatula, until browned, about 10 minutes. Stir in the miso paste, sambal oelek, and soy sauce. Add the broth and bring to a simmer, then reduce the heat to medium-low and continue gently simmering until ready to serve.

2 When you're just about ready to serve the soup, add the frozen corn, scallions, and ramen (discarding any spice packets that come with the ramen). Simmer until the noodles are tender, about 10 minutes.

3 Use tongs to divide the noodles among bowls, then ladle the hot soup on top and garnish with sliced bamboo shoots, fresh bean sprouts, and dried seaweed, as desired.

SHEPHERD'S POT PIE

SERVES 4 TO 6

THIS DISH IS WHAT HAPPENS WHEN SHEP-herd's pie and pot pie bunk up under the same (Dutch oven) roof. The usual shepherd's pie suspects are all in attendance—ground lamb, creamy pota-toes, carrots, plenty of Worcestershire, and bright peas—but instead of a mashed potato cap, we're simplifying things by topping the dish with a store-bought puff pastry crust! The end result is less time-consuming, but just as satisfying (and maybe even more beautiful) than the original.

2 pounds ground lamb

4 Yukon Gold potatoes, cut into ¾-inch pieces

3 medium carrots, peeled and chopped

3 stalks celery, chopped

1 shallot, chopped

2 cups beef broth

3 tablespoons tomato paste

2 tablespoons Worcestershire sauce

1 tablespoon chopped fresh thyme leaves

1 teaspoon kosher salt

½ teaspoon ground black pepper

1 cup frozen peas

1 sheet frozen puff pastry (from a 17.3-ounce package), thawed (see tip, page 88)

1 Preheat the oven to 400°F, with a rack in the center position.

2 Cook the lamb in a medium (5- to 6-quart) Dutch oven over medium-high heat, breaking it up with a wooden spoon or spatula, until browned, about 10 minutes. Add the potatoes, carrots, celery, and shallot and cook until the vegetables are tender, 10 to 15 minutes. Stir in the broth, tomato paste, Worcestershire, thyme, salt, and pepper and bring to a simmer. Simmer for 5 minutes, then remove from the heat. Stir in the frozen peas.

3 Cut 3 large slits in the puff pastry and drape the pastry over the stew, folding the edges up the sides of the pot. Transfer the pot to the oven and bake until the crust is deeply golden brown all over, about 25 minutes.

4 Allow to cool slightly before scooping out and serv-ing hot.

CHAPTER SEVEN

SWEETS

4 cups fresh (or frozen) mixed berries

1 cup crème fraîche

1 cup heavy cream

½ teaspoon grated lemon zest

½ teaspoon pure vanilla extract

2 tablespoons granulated sugar

¼ cup packed light brown sugar

BROILED
BERRIES & CREAM

SERVES 4

THIS CARAMELIZED DELIGHT IS AS SIMPLE AS it gets. We'll toss fresh berries in a pan, douse them in a creamy, lemony, lightly sweet dairy mixture, sprinkle the whole thing with brown sugar, and then let the broiler do its magic. The resulting skillet is like a mix between berries and cream and crème brûlée, and it's a smart and surprising delight.

1   Preheat the oven to broil, with a rack about 4 inches from the heat and another rack in the bottom position. Place a sheet of foil (or a sheet pan) on the bottom rack (to catch any drips).

2   Arrange the berries in an even layer in a 10-inch cast iron skillet.

3   In a medium bowl, whisk together the crème fraîche, heavy cream, lemon zest, vanilla, and granulated sugar until smooth. Pour the cream mixture over the berries, letting it seep into all of the crevices in the pan. Sprinkle the brown sugar evenly on top.

4   Place the pan under the broiler and broil, keeping a close eye to prevent burning or overflow, until the brown sugar has caramelized and the custard mixture is thick and bubbling, 3 to 6 minutes.

5   Serve immediately.

SUBBING OUT

If you want to go off the one-pan grid and make this in a few small ramekins instead of a large skillet, you certainly can! Just be sure they aren't too deep—shallow vessels are best for producing the perfect, caramelized texture.

WARM APPLE BISCUIT CAKE

THIS IS SORT OF THE DESSERT VERSION OF the already-sweet monkey bread, stuffed with buttery, gently spiced apple and cinnamon-scented caramelized sugar. If you wanted to serve this with big scoops of vanilla bean ice cream in the center of the Bundt ring, I certainly wouldn't be the one to stop you.

1 Granny Smith apple, peeled, cored, and very thinly sliced (about 2 cups)

¼ cup granulated sugar

¼ teaspoon ground cardamom

1 tablespoon fresh lemon juice

8 tablespoons (1 stick) unsalted butter, melted and cooled, plus more for greasing the pan

1 cup packed dark brown sugar

5 teaspoons ground cinnamon

2 (8-ounce) cans store-bought refrigerated buttermilk biscuit dough, biscuits quartered, or homemade dough (see opposite)

1 Preheat the oven to 350°F.

2 In a medium bowl, stir together the apple slices, granulated sugar, cardamom, and lemon juice. Pour the melted butter into a small bowl. In another medium bowl, stir together the brown sugar and cinnamon.

3 Grease a 12-cup Bundt pan with butter or cooking spray. Arrange a layer of sugared apples in the bottom of the pan.

4 Dunk each piece of dough into the melted butter, then roll in the brown sugar–cinnamon mixture. Place the coated dough balls over the apples in the Bundt pan, spacing them about ½ inch apart. Continue alternating layers of sugary apples and dough in the pan. When the dough has been used up, mix any remaining butter and brown sugar together and pour it over the dough in the pan.

5 Bake until fragrant and very brown, with a dark, sugary crust, 30 to 40 minutes.

6 Allow the cake to cool in the pan for about 15 minutes before carefully inverting onto a large plate or serving platter. The cake is best served warm from the oven.

DIY DOUGH!

WHEN I HAVE TIME, I LOVE MAKING THIS tender, fluffy dough from scratch. Here's how:

2 teaspoons rapid-rise yeast

1⅓ cups barely warm water

2 tablespoons extra virgin olive oil

2 tablespoons honey

3½ cups all-purpose flour

2 teaspoons kosher salt

1 In a large bowl (or in a stand mixer fitted with the dough hook), mix the yeast and water together and let it sit for 5 minutes. Stir in the olive oil, honey, flour, and salt to form a dough. With well-floured hands (or the dough hook), knead the dough until cohesive and elastic.

2 Transfer the dough to a large bowl misted with cooking spray. Cover with a clean kitchen towel and allow the dough to sit in a warm corner of the kitchen until doubled in size, about 1 hour.

3 When the dough has doubled in size, flour your hands, punch it down, and break off pieces the size of golf balls, rolling each into a smooth ball. Dunk the dough balls in the butter and sugar and layer them in the pan, according to the recipe's instructions. Then cover the Bundt pan with a clean kitchen towel and let the dough rise once more, this time for 15 to 20 minutes, before baking as instructed.

CHOCOLATE MOLTEN CARAMEL MINI CAKES

⌐ MAKES 12 MINI CAKES ⌐

REMEMBER IN THE '90S, WHEN MOLTEN LAVA cakes were all the rage? Why did they fall out of fashion? As far as I can tell, there's absolutely nothing wrong with a personal-size cake that oozes warm, chocolaty goodness from its center. I mean, flannel shirts and dark lipstick have already come back around—what are we waiting for on this cake?! Using store-bought chocolate caramel truffles for the oozy center is a fun sort of hack, and the resulting little cakes are just heavenly.

6 tablespoons unsalted butter, plus more for greasing the pan

Unsweetened cocoa powder, for dusting the pan

8 ounces bittersweet chocolate chips

½ teaspoon espresso powder

4 large eggs

½ cup sugar

1 teaspoon pure vanilla extract

½ teaspoon kosher salt

¼ cup all-purpose flour

12 chocolate caramel truffles

Flaky sea salt, to finish

Ice cream or whipped cream, for serving

1 Preheat the oven to 400°F, with a rack in the center position. Grease a 12-cup muffin tin with butter and dust lightly with cocoa powder, tapping out any excess.

2 In the microwave or double boiler (see tip, opposite), melt the chocolate chips with the espresso powder and butter, stirring until smooth. Allow to cool for 10 minutes.

3 In a large bowl using an electric mixer, beat the eggs with the sugar on high speed until thickened and doubled in volume. Beat in the vanilla and kosher salt. Sift the flour into the batter. Add the melted chocolate mixture and fold gently to combine.

4 Divide the batter among the prepared muffin cups. Drop one caramel truffle into each cup, pressing it down into the batter to fully submerge. Sprinkle each cake with a pinch of flaky sea salt.

5 Transfer the cakes to the oven and bake until the tops are set, about 11 minutes. Remove and allow them to cool for 5 to 10 minutes, then quickly and carefully invert the pan to release the cakes from the muffin tin.

6 Serve the cakes warm, with a scoop of ice cream or whipped cream alongside.

HOW TO?
USE A DOUBLE
BOILER

A double boiler is simply a heatproof bowl set above a small pot of simmering water. The simmering water creates steam that heats the bowl's contents (in this case, chocolate chips) gently and evenly, so there's no need to worry about scorching or curdling. You can buy pots marketed as double boilers (which look like two, stacked pots) at most kitchen stores, but it's easy to create your own with a small pot and a medium glass or metal bowl set atop. Just be sure that the water in the pot doesn't actually touch the bottom of the bowl; it should simmer about an inch below.

PEACH & POLENTA CAKE

WHEN PEACHES ARE IN SEASON, I'M HARD pressed to eat them in any other way than standing over the sink, sweet juice dripping down my chin, but in this cake the floral fruit pairs perfectly with sweet polenta. The polenta and dried fruit soak up the peach juices and produce a beautifully moist, tender cake, perfect on its own, dusted with powdered sugar, or dolloped with a bit of crème fraîche. This cake can be stored, refrigerated or at room temperature, for about 2 days.

½ cup granulated sugar

¼ teaspoon ground cinnamon

2 medium peaches, pitted and each cut into 8 wedges

¾ cup all-purpose flour

½ cup polenta

1 teaspoon baking powder

¼ teaspoon kosher salt

8 tablespoons (1 stick) unsalted butter, at room temperature

¼ cup packed light brown sugar

2 large eggs, at room temperature

2 tablespoons sour cream

1 teaspoon pure vanilla extract

⅓ cup dried peaches or apricots, finely chopped

1 Preheat the oven to 350°F. Grease a 9-inch tart pan with cooking spray or butter.

2 In a medium bowl, combine ¼ cup of the granulated sugar and the cinnamon. Set aside 2 tablespoons of the mixture. Add the peach wedges to the remainder and toss to coat.

3 In a separate medium bowl, whisk together the flour, polenta, baking powder, and salt.

4 In a large bowl using an electric mixer, cream the butter, brown sugar, and remaining ¼ cup granulated sugar on medium speed until light and fluffy. Add the eggs, one at a time, mixing well, then add the sour cream and vanilla and beat to combine. With the mixer on low speed, add the flour mixture and mix just until homogeneous.

5 Pour the batter into the prepared pan and spread it evenly. Scatter with the dried fruit, arrange the peaches in a circular pattern, and sprinkle with the reserved cinnamon sugar.

6 Bake until a tester inserted into the center comes out clean, 35 to 45 minutes.

7 Allow the cake to cool for 1 hour before slicing and serving warm or at room temperature.

SKILLET
BROWNIE
SUNDAE

◦ SERVES 4 TO 6 ◦

I ALMOST DON'T WANT TO TELL YOU ABOUT this giant, warm brownie smothered in ice cream and sundae toppings, because then I might have to share. But I will. This brownie batter is built right in the skillet, then baked off until it's just underdone—at which point we're ready for an obscenity of toppings. Anything goes—go nuts (or caramel, whipped cream, fudge sauce, and maraschino cherries), if you want to!

10 tablespoons unsalted butter

8 ounces bittersweet chocolate chips

1 cup sugar

3 large eggs

1 teaspoon pure vanilla extract

½ cup plus 2 tablespoons all-purpose flour

2 tablespoons unsweetened cocoa powder

½ teaspoon kosher salt

Ice cream, caramel sauce, and sprinkles, for serving

1 Preheat the oven to 350°F, with a rack in the center position.

2 Melt the butter in a 10-inch cast iron skillet over medium heat. Remove from the heat and add the chocolate chips, stirring them into the butter until fully melted.

3 Whisk in the sugar. When the chocolate mixture is no longer hot to the touch, about 15 minutes, whisk in the eggs, one at a time, and then the vanilla. Add the flour, cocoa powder, and salt and mix gently, just until incorporated. Use a rubber spatula to scrape down the sides of the pan and smooth out the batter.

4 Transfer the skillet to the oven and bake until a skewer inserted into the center comes out with a few moist crumbs, 25 to 30 minutes. (Do not overbake! Err on the underbaked side, if you're not sure.)

5 Remove the skillet from the oven and allow the brownie to cool for 10 minutes, then top it with generous scoops of ice cream, caramel sauce, and sprinkles. Serve it warm, straight from the pan.

CHEWY CHOCOLATE HAZELNUT COOKIES

⊹ MAKES 1 DOZEN ⊹

ARE YOU THE KIND OF PERSON WHO COULD sit down with a tub of chocolate hazelnut spread and a spoon and be perfectly happy for an hour or so? Yes? Let's be friends. I made these cookies for you! Just five ingredients, and you're well on your way to crisp-edged, soft-centered chocolaty hazelnut cookies. You'll want these with a big glass of cold milk alongside.

1 cup chocolate hazelnut spread (I like Nutella)
1 large egg
½ cup all-purpose flour
1 teaspoon kosher salt
½ cup hazelnuts, coarsely ground

1   Preheat the oven to 350°F, with a rack in the center position. Line a sheet pan with parchment paper.

2   In a large bowl, mix together the chocolate hazelnut spread and egg until smooth. Add the flour and salt, mixing well to combine.

3   Scoop the batter into 2-inch balls and roll each ball in the ground hazelnuts. Arrange the dough balls on the prepared sheet pan, leaving an inch or two in between. Press the dough gently to flatten the tops.

4   Transfer the cookies to the oven and bake until the tops are slightly crackled, the hazelnuts are golden, and the cookies look mostly dry, 8 to 12 minutes.

5   Remove the cookies from the oven and allow them to cool on the pan for about 10 minutes before serving slightly warm or at room temperature.

CHOCOLATE ROSEMARY SHORTBREAD TART

SERVES 16

DARK CHOCOLATE PAIRS BEAUTIFULLY WITH fresh rosemary and sea salt in this classed-up shortbread tart. It finishes incredibly dense and rich, so slice it thinly and serve it with some fresh whipped cream (only lightly sweetened) or scoops of ice cream alongside.

2 sticks (8 ounces) unsalted butter, at room temperature

1 cup powdered sugar

1 teaspoon chopped fresh rosemary, plus more for garnish

2 teaspoons pure vanilla extract

1 teaspoon kosher salt

1½ cups all-purpose flour

½ cup unsweetened cocoa powder

½ cup bittersweet chocolate chips

½ teaspoon sea salt

1 In a large bowl using an electric mixer, cream the butter, sugar, and rosemary until smooth and fluffy. Beat in the vanilla and kosher salt.

2 Sift together the flour and cocoa powder, then add it to the butter mixture, mixing gently until a crumbly dough just comes together. Press the dough into a 9-inch tart pan. Transfer the pan to the refrigerator to chill for at least 15 minutes.

3 Preheat the oven to 350°F, with a rack in the center position.

4 Remove the dough from the refrigerator and gently prick it all over with a fork. Transfer it to the oven and bake until the tart is dry and set (it will bubble slightly at the top), about 15 minutes. Scatter the chocolate chips over the hot tart and return to the oven for 2 minutes to melt the chips.

5 Meanwhile, in a small bowl, mix the extra chopped rosemary together with the sea salt.

6 Remove the tart from the oven and use a spatula to spread the melted chocolate evenly over the tart. Sprinkle the herby salt evenly over the melted chocolate. Allow the tart to cool and the chocolate to set, about 30 minutes, before slicing it very thinly into wedges and serving at room temperature.

CONFETTI
PAVLOVA

> SERVES 6 <

IN MY MIND, SPRINKLES ARE ALWAYS A GOOD idea. And even a classy, elegant dessert like Pavlova—which sounds fancy, but is just a baked meringue topped with whipped cream and berries—needs a confetti of sprinkles thrown in every now and again. The meringue is cooked low and slow in the oven to achieve a crisp crust and a slightly moist, tender interior. Plan ahead and make this either in the morning or the night before you want to serve it. Let's confetti the heck out of this one!

5 large egg whites, at room temperature

½ teaspoon kosher salt

¾ cup plus 1 tablespoon sugar

2 teaspoons cornstarch

1 teaspoon pure vanilla extract

1 cup rainbow sprinkles, plus more for topping

1 cup heavy cream

1 cup raspberries

1 Preheat the oven to 300°F, with a rack in the center position. Line a sheet pan with parchment paper.

2 In a stand mixer fitted with the whisk attachment, beat the egg whites and salt on high speed until white and foamy, about 1 minute. With the mixer still on high, gradually add ¾ cup of the sugar, beating until firm, shiny peaks form.

3 Remove the bowl from the mixer and sift the cornstarch on top. Add the vanilla and sprinkles and fold gently until combined.

4 Pile the meringue onto the prepared sheet pan, spreading it out with a spatula to form a large (roughly 9-inch) round of meringue.

5 Transfer the pan to the oven and immediately reduce the heat to 250°F. Bake the meringue for 2 hours, then turn off the oven and allow the meringue to cool in the oven for at least 1 hour and up to overnight.

6 When you're ready to serve, carefully remove the baked meringue from the parchment and place it on a serving platter.

7 In a large bowl using an electric mixer (or a whisk and some arm strength), whip the heavy cream with the remaining 1 tablespoon sugar until soft peaks form. Spread the whipped cream over the meringue and top with fresh berries and an extra scattering of rainbow sprinkles.

8 Slice or spoon into large wedges and serve immediately.

BLACKBERRY OAT CRISP

> SERVES 8 TO 10

8 cups fresh (or frozen) blackberries

1½ cups granulated sugar

1¼ cups all-purpose flour

1 tablespoon grated lemon zest (from about 1 lemon)

¼ cup fresh lemon juice (from about 1 lemon)

1 teaspoon pure vanilla extract

2 cups old-fashioned rolled oats

1 cup packed light brown sugar

¼ teaspoon ground cinnamon

1 teaspoon kosher salt

2 sticks (8 ounces) unsalted butter, melted and cooled

Vanilla ice cream or heavy cream, for serving (optional)

IN THE SUMMER, WILD BLACKBERRIES GROW so profusely in Seattle that you can stop and pick them along stretches of the highway, although I wouldn't necessarily recommend braving wildly speeding cars to get a handful. What better to do with all those berries than make a sweet treat? This buttery, oat-topped blackberry crisp is one of my go-to summer desserts, although, lucky for us, it's easily made in the winter with frozen berries instead of fresh. A splash of fresh cream or scoop of vanilla ice cream on the side is only sort of optional.

1 Preheat the oven to 350°F, with a rack in the center position.

2 Toss the blackberries in a 9 × 13-inch baking dish with ½ cup of the granulated sugar, ¼ cup of the flour, the lemon zest, lemon juice, and vanilla.

3 In a medium bowl, whisk together the oats, brown sugar, remaining 1 cup flour and 1 cup sugar, the cinnamon, and salt. Pour the melted butter over the flour mixture and stir until it's clumpy yet cohesive.

4 Scatter the oat crumble thickly over the blackberries, transfer the crisp to the oven, and bake until the top is deeply golden brown and the berries are bubbling, 45 minutes to 1 hour.

5 Serve the crisp warm, with scoops of vanilla ice cream or a glug of fresh cream alongside, if you like.

CHOCOLATE CHIP
CHEESECAKE SQUARES

SERVES 12 TO 15

THESE LITTLE CHEESECAKE SQUARES, CHOCK-full of mini chips, are what I wish I had in my lunch box every day in elementary school. (My mom usually just packed me an apple or orange as a "treat." Thanks, Mama.) They're ultra creamy and a little bit nostalgic, somehow, with a chocolate cookie crust, rich vanilla flavor, and plenty of chocolate flecked throughout.

11 ounces (about 26) chocolate sandwich cookies (I like Oreos)

6 tablespoons unsalted butter, melted

1 pound full-fat cream cheese

1 cup packed light brown sugar

15 ounces whole-milk ricotta cheese

3 large eggs

2 teaspoons pure vanilla extract

½ teaspoon kosher salt

1 cup mini chocolate chips

16 ounces full-fat sour cream

3 tablespoons granulated sugar

1 Preheat the oven to 350°F, with a rack in the center position.

2 In a food processor, pulse the cookies and melted butter together until fine crumbs form. Press the crumbs into an even layer in the bottom of a 9 × 13-inch baking dish. Scrape the food processor as clean of crumbs as you can manage.

3 Add the cream cheese and brown sugar to the food processor and pulse until creamy and smooth. Add the ricotta, eggs, 1 teaspoon of the vanilla, and the salt and pulse until velvety.

4 Stir the chocolate chips into the cream cheese mixture and pour the filling over the cookie crust, smoothing the top in an even layer with a spatula. Transfer to the oven and bake until the cheesecake is mostly set (it will jiggle softly like Jell-O), about 40 minutes.

5 While the cheesecake bakes, in a medium bowl, whisk together the sour cream, granulated sugar, and remaining 1 teaspoon vanilla.

6 Remove the cheesecake from the oven and spread the sour cream mixture over the almost-set cheesecake bars. Return to the oven and continue baking until just slightly jiggly in the center, about 10 minutes.

7 Allow the cheesecake to cool completely (a few hours in the refrigerator should do it) before slicing into squares and serving.

GRAMMA'S
BANANA CAKE
WITH
PEANUT BUTTER FROSTING

◦ SERVES 8 TO 10 ◦

THIS IS MY GRAMMA INEZ'S RECIPE, AND AT nearly ninety years old, Grams is still playing tennis weekly, ripping through the *New York Times* Sunday crossword puzzle, and dominating at mah-jongg. Clearly, we've all got a lot to learn. Inez's banana cake is springy and tender, and with five (!) whole bananas inside, doesn't want for sweet flavor. A quickly whipped peanut butter frosting is the perfect topper, though sometimes Gramma just dusts the naked cake with a little powdered sugar and calls it a day. However you choose to serve it, you'll want to brush up on your mah-jongg, because she's coming for you.

FOR THE CAKE

5 ripe bananas

¼ cup buttermilk

1 tablespoon baking soda

1 teaspoon kosher salt

2 sticks (8 ounces) unsalted butter, melted and cooled

1½ cups granulated sugar

3 large eggs

1 teaspoon pure vanilla extract

2 cups all-purpose flour

1 cup chopped nuts or chocolate chips, plus more for decorating (optional)

FOR THE FROSTING

8 ounces full-fat cream cheese

8 tablespoons (1 stick) unsalted butter, at room temperature

4 cups powdered sugar

⅔ cup creamy peanut butter

Kosher salt

1 Preheat the oven to 350°F. Grease and flour a 12-cup Bundt pan.

2 To make the cake: In a food processor or blender, blend the bananas, buttermilk, baking soda, and salt until smooth and slightly bubbly.

3 In a large bowl, whisk together the melted butter, granulated sugar, eggs, and vanilla. Alternately add the flour and the banana mixture to this mixture, beginning and ending with the flour, stirring gently to incorporate after each addition. Fold in the chopped nuts or chocolate chips, if using.

4 Pour the batter into the prepared Bundt pan, transfer to the oven, and bake until a tester inserted into the center of the cake comes out clean, 45 minutes to 1 hour. Allow the cake to cool for 30 minutes in the pan before carefully inverting onto a wire rack to finish cooling completely.

RECIPE CONTINUES

5 While the cake cools, make the frosting: In a bowl, with an electric mixer, beat the cream cheese and butter together until very smooth. Slowly beat in the powdered sugar, about ½ cup at a time, until silky. Add the peanut butter and a pinch of salt and mix well to combine. Taste the frosting and adjust; if you want more PB flavor, add more, 1 or 2 tablespoons at a time. If you'd like a sweeter frosting, slowly incorporate more powdered sugar.

6 When the cake is completely cool, use a serrated knife to slice it in half horizontally. Spread half of the frosting on the bottom layer, and carefully set the top layer over the frosting. Slather the top layer with the remaining frosting. (Alternatively, you could skip the layering and just spread the frosting over the top of the cake.) Sprinkle a few chopped nuts or chocolate chips on top to decorate, if you like.

7 Slice the cake into thick wedges to serve.

OATMEAL CARAMEL COOKIE THINS

SERVES 12 TO 15

I'M USUALLY A CHOCOLATE-IN-MY-COOKIES kind of gal, but for brown-sugary, caramel-packed bars, I'll make an exception. The dough for these almost butterscotch-flavored treats comes together in mere minutes, and instead of scooping it into cookies, we'll just press it out into the bottom of a baking dish. A caramel bath follows, and the result is a crisp-bottomed, gooey oat bar.

1½ cups all-purpose flour

1½ cups old-fashioned rolled oats

1 cup packed dark brown sugar

¾ teaspoon baking soda

1 teaspoon kosher salt

1 stick plus 1 tablespoon unsalted butter, melted

1 cup good caramel sauce (I like Trader Joe's or Fran's)

1 Preheat the oven to 350°F, with a rack in the center position. Mist a 9 × 13-inch baking dish with cooking spray, line it with an overhang of parchment paper, and mist the parchment, too.

2 In a medium bowl, whisk together the flour, oats, brown sugar, baking soda, and salt. Add the melted butter and stir until a clumpy dough forms.

3 Press three-fourths of the cookie dough into the bottom of the prepared pan. Transfer to the oven and bake until the cookie is just starting to brown, 10 to 12 minutes.

4 Remove the pan from the oven (leave the oven on) and spread the caramel sauce over the warm cookie layer. Crumble the remaining cookie dough on top of the caramel layer, return the pan to the oven, and bake until deeply golden brown, about 15 minutes.

5 Remove and allow to cool completely, about 45 minutes, before using the parchment overhang to lift the cookie out of the pan and transfer it to a cutting board. Cut into squares or rectangles and serve.

HOW TO? MAKE HOMEMADE CARAMEL

There are a number of excellent store-bought options out there, but if you'd like to make your own caramel sauce, here's how: In a medium saucepan, melt 1 cup sugar over medium heat, stirring constantly, until amber in color. Immediately stir in 6 tablespoons salted butter (the mixture will bubble up), then slowly whisk in ½ cup heavy cream (again, the mixture will bubble and splatter—stand back!). Boil the caramel for 1 minute, then remove from the heat and stir in a big pinch of sea salt. Allow the caramel to cool, about 1 hour, before using it (it will thicken as it cools).

MACAROON CHOCOLATE BARK

SERVES 15 TO 20

HERE'S A FUN WAY TO GET THE SWEET, COCO-nutty flavor of macaroons, without going to the trouble of scooping and shaping all those little cookies. We'll just spread the coconut mixture on a sheet pan and bake it until golden, then top it with a layer of chocolate chips, which will melt and become beautifully spreadable. And best of all, since we're making bark instead of cookies, we get to go bananas with toppings! From a simple sprinkle of sea salt to a hurricane of chopped candies, crushed pretzels, and/or dried fruit, there's no wrong way to play this game.

14 ounces sweetened flaked coconut (about 3½ cups)

⅔ cup sugar

3 large egg whites

½ teaspoon kosher salt

½ teaspoon almond extract

2 cups bittersweet chocolate chips

Flaky sea salt, sprinkles, chopped candies, or crushed pretzels, for topping

1   Preheat the oven to 325°F, with a rack in the center position. Line a sheet pan with parchment paper.

2   In a food processor, pulse together the coconut and sugar until well combined. Add the egg whites, salt, and almond extract and pulse until fluffy and smooth.

3   Spread the coconut mixture onto the prepared sheet pan, using a spatula to smooth it out into an even ¼- to ½-inch-thick layer. Transfer it to the oven and bake until dry and golden brown, 10 to 15 minutes.

4   Remove the pan from the oven and immediately sprinkle the chocolate chips over the coconut layer. Return the pan to the oven for 3 to 5 minutes more to melt the chips. Remove the pan from the oven and spread the melted chocolate evenly over the coconut layer with an offset spatula.

5   Press your desired toppings into the melted chocolate, then let the bark cool completely (I recommend sticking it in the refrigerator for about 30 minutes) before slicing it into rough squares and serving.

COOKIES 'N' CREAM

UPSIDE-DOWN CAKE

SERVES 8

THIS CAKE IS A HUMBLE, ONE-LAYER AFFAIR, but don't be fooled—there's enough richness here for Donald Trump *and* Kanye. We're studding standard white cake batter, springy and tender on its own, with dark, crunchy cookie pieces. Cookies 'n' cream meets cake! Layering whole cookies on the bottom of the pan leaves a fun pattern on the final, upturned surface and renders frosting a moot point. The only things this cake wants are a dollop of whipped cream and a tall glass of milk with which to wash it down.

1 box (14.3 ounces) Oreos or other chocolate sandwich cookie

1 cup plus 2 tablespoons cake flour

1¼ cups plus 2 tablespoons sugar

2 teaspoons baking powder

½ teaspoon kosher salt

6 tablespoons unsalted butter, cubed, at room temperature

½ cup milk, at room temperature

3 large egg whites, at room temperature

½ teaspoon pure vanilla extract

1 Preheat the oven to 350°F. Mist a 9-inch cake pan with cooking spray, line it with parchment paper, and mist the parchment, too.

2 Arrange a layer of cookies in the bottom of the pan (break—or nibble—a few to fit, if necessary). Place about 12 more cookies in a plastic bag and crush gently, until you've got a good cup of cookie crumbs. Set aside.

3 In the bowl of a stand mixer fitted with the paddle attachment, mix together the cake flour, sugar, baking powder, and salt. Add the butter and mix on low speed for 3 to 5 minutes until fully incorporated.

4 In a medium bowl, whisk together the milk, egg whites, and vanilla. Slowly add the milk mixture to the flour and mix for 1 to 2 minutes until smooth. Fold in the reserved cookie crumbs.

5 Pour the cake batter into the pan and spread evenly with a spatula to smooth the top. Transfer to the oven and bake until a tester inserted into the center of the cake comes out clean, 30 to 35 minutes.

6 Allow the cake to cool in the pan for about 30 minutes before inverting onto a serving platter and letting cool completely.

7 Slice the cake into wedges and serve at room temperature.

BRÛLÉED POUND CAKE WITH CITRUS

⊱ SERVES 4 TO 6 ⊰

THIS DESSERT IS KIND OF LIKE CHEATING. That is, if you consider doctoring store-bought pound cake into a simple and classy dessert cheating. I call it "being human, and probably a genius, too." No shame, people! You slice that pound cake proudly. Go ahead and slather it with sweet, tangy sour cream custard, and top it with bright slices of citrus. You're about to get your *brûlée* on. I like to use a mix of navel and Cara Cara oranges, to vary up the flavor and color combo of the finished dish, but use whatever citrus you like best.

1 loaf (16 ounces) store-bought pound cake

2 cups full-fat sour cream

2 tablespoons dark brown sugar

¼ teaspoon kosher salt

2 or 3 oranges, peeled, halved, and sliced into rounds

2 tablespoons granulated sugar

1 Preheat the oven to broil, with a rack about 4 inches from the heat. Mist a sheet pan with cooking spray.

2 Cut the pound cake into 1-inch-thick slices and evenly arrange them cut-side up on the sheet pan.

3 In a small bowl, whisk together the sour cream, brown sugar, and salt. Dollop a big spoonful of the mixture over each slice of pound cake, leaving the short edges of the cake bare. Top the sour cream layer with a slice or two of orange, and sprinkle the granulated sugar evenly over the fruit.

4 Transfer to the oven and broil, keeping a close eye on the pan to prevent burning, until the pound cake edges are charred and the oranges are deeply caramelized, about 3 minutes.

5 Serve the pound cake warm, with any leftover sweetened sour cream alongside.

GIANT COOKIE CAKE

> SERVES 6 TO 8

REMEMBER THOSE HUGE, CIRCULAR CHOCO-late chip cookie "cakes" from the super-market? The ones with a scalloped edge of brightly colored frosting that got cut into little wedges and served at the ele-mentary school book fair? Well. This is our own, homemade-in-a-skillet ver-sion, without the sickly sweet swirls of artificial frosting on top (although if you wanted to let this fully cool and then pipe on something lightly sweet, you'd have my full support). It's rich and indul-gent and, frosted or not, makes a pretty cute birthday or special occasion "cake."

6 tablespoons unsalted butter, at room temperature

½ cup packed dark brown sugar

⅓ cup granulated sugar

1 large egg

1 teaspoon pure vanilla extract

1 cup all-purpose flour

½ teaspoon baking soda

½ teaspoon kosher salt

1 cup bittersweet chocolate chips

Pinch of flaky sea salt

1 Preheat the oven to 350°F, with a rack in the center position.

2 In a large bowl using an electric mixer, cream the butter and sugars together until fluffy and smooth. Beat in the egg and vanilla until incorporated. Add the flour, baking soda, and kosher salt and stir until the cookie dough just comes together. Fold in the chocolate chips.

3 Spread the cookie dough evenly into a 10-inch cast iron skillet and sprinkle the top with the sea salt. Transfer the pan to the oven and bake until the cookie is golden brown on top and just cooked through, about 20 minutes.

4 Allow to cool for about 5 minutes before slicing into wedges and serving warm.

PEAR HALVES
WITH
CRUMBLE
TOPS

⤙ SERVES 4 TO 6 ⤚

WE'RE BUILDING LITTLE PERSONAL PEAR crumbles here. In fact, the pears themselves *are* the crumble! That is, the buttery topping gets piled directly onto the pear halves—no pesky peeling or chopping required—and then baked to slumpy, toasted perfection. The pears release their juices and soak up the beautiful crumble, and in the end all the dish needs is a giant scoop of ice cream (or even Greek yogurt, if you wanted to serve this for breakfast—which would be a great call, by the way).

4 ripe pears (I like Bosc or Anjou), halved and cored
Juice of 1 lemon
½ cup almond meal
¼ cup sugar
¼ cup old-fashioned rolled oats
½ teaspoon ground cinnamon
¼ teaspoon kosher salt
4 tablespoons cold unsalted butter, cubed
Ice cream or Greek yogurt, for serving

1 Preheat the oven to 350°F, with a rack in the center position. Grease a 9 × 13-inch baking dish with cooking spray or butter.

2 Arrange the pear halves cut-side up in the prepared baking dish. Squeeze the lemon juice on top.

3 In a medium bowl, whisk together the almond meal, sugar, oats, cinnamon, and salt. Add the butter and work it in with your fingers until a rough and crumbly dough comes together.

4 Pile the crumble mixture onto the pears, about ¼ cup of topping per pear half. Transfer to the oven and bake until the pears are fork-tender and the topping is browned and crisp, 45 minutes to 1 hour.

5 Serve the pears warm or at room temperature, with scoops of ice cream or Greek yogurt on top.

S'MORES CUPS

◁ MAKES 12 CUPS ▷

8 tablespoons (1 stick) unsalted butter, at room temperature, plus more for greasing the tins

¾ cup packed light brown sugar

1 teaspoon pure vanilla extract

1 large egg

1 cup all-purpose flour

1 cup finely processed graham cracker crumbs

½ teaspoon baking powder

¾ cup marshmallow creme (I like Fluff)

½ cup bittersweet chocolate chips

Flaky sea salt

THESE CUTE LITTLE CUPS WILL HAVE EVERYONE begging for s'more. (Sorry. Had to.) They start with a graham cracker–infused short dough, which gets layered with marshmallow creme, bittersweet chocolate chips, and a pinch of salt to temper the sweetness. Traditional? Not so much. Playful and delicious? Bad puns and all, you bet.

1 Preheat the oven to 350°F, with a rack in the center position. Grease a 12-cup muffin tin with cooking spray or butter.

2 In a large bowl using an electric mixer, cream together the butter and brown sugar until light and fluffy. Beat in the vanilla and egg.

3 In a smaller bowl, stir together the flour, graham cracker crumbs, and baking powder. Add the dry ingredients to the butter-sugar mixture and mix gently until just combined.

4 Measure out ½ cup of the dough and set aside for the topping. Press the remainder evenly into the prepared muffin cups, filling each about one-fourth full.

5 Spoon 1 tablespoon of the marshmallow creme over each cup, then top with a sprinkle of chocolate chips, dividing them evenly among the cups. Crumble the reserved dough over the chocolate chips, and top each cup with a pinch of sea salt.

6 Transfer to the oven and bake until the marshmallow creme is puffed and the dough is deeply golden brown, about 15 minutes.

7 Allow the cups to cool slightly before running a paring knife around the edges of each one to pop out of the pan. Serve warm or at room temperature.

PORT-ROASTED NECTARINES

IF YOU HAVEN'T YET FOUND AN EXCUSE TO go out and buy some port, consider this as good a reason as any. Smooth and slightly sweet, the fortified wine mixes beautifully here with butter, honey, nutmeg, and salt to make a rich roasting base for bright, succulent nectarines. A spoonful of whipped cream or some vanilla ice cream makes a cool, refreshing topper. Plums are a good substitute for nectarines, if you're so inclined.

3 tablespoons unsalted butter

½ cup port

⅓ cup honey

Pinch of ground nutmeg

Pinch of kosher salt

4 large nectarines, halved and pitted

Vanilla ice cream or whipped cream, for serving

1 Preheat the oven to 400°F, with a rack in the center position.

2 Place the butter in a 9 × 13-inch baking dish and transfer it to the oven to melt the butter, 3 to 5 minutes.

3 Remove the pan from the oven and add the port, honey, nutmeg, and salt and stir to combine. Arrange the fruit cut-side down in the pan. Return to the oven and bake until the nectarines are very tender and have released some of their juices, 25 to 30 minutes. In the last 10 minutes of baking, turn the nectarines over and baste them with the liquid in the pan.

4 Serve the nectarines warm, topped with big scoops of vanilla ice cream or whipped cream.

HALFWAY COOKIE BITES

HALF COOKIE BAR, HALF MARSHMALLOWY, brown sugar meringue, these little "halfway" squares, made popular in the 1950s and '60s, are all the way wonderful. A layer of chocolate chips between the cookie base and the meringue topping is traditional, but I've seen versions that skip the chocolate and use fruit jam or butterscotch chips instead. (Personally, I vote chocolate, but you do what feels best for you.)

---

2 cups all-purpose flour

1 teaspoon baking powder

¼ teaspoon baking soda

1 teaspoon kosher salt

8 tablespoons (1 stick) unsalted butter, at room temperature

½ cup granulated sugar

1 cup packed light brown sugar

2 large eggs, separated

1 large egg white

2 teaspoons pure vanilla extract

12 ounces semisweet chocolate chips

1 Preheat the oven to 350°F, with a rack in the center position. Mist a 9 × 13-inch baking dish with cooking spray, line it with parchment paper, letting it overhang the dish on opposite sides, and mist the parchment, too.

2 In a medium bowl, whisk together the flour, baking powder, baking soda, and salt.

3 In the bowl of a stand mixer fitted with the paddle attachment, cream together the butter, granulated sugar, and ½ cup of the brown sugar until smooth and fluffy. Add the egg yolks, beating them in to combine. Beat in the vanilla.

4 Add the flour mixture and mix gently, until a crumbly dough just comes together. Press the dough as evenly as possible into the bottom of the prepared pan. Scatter the chocolate chips evenly over the cookie dough, pressing them gently to adhere.

5 In the clean bowl of a stand mixer fitted with the whisk attachment, whip the 3 egg whites at medium-high speed until very frothy and white. Slowly add the remaining ½ cup brown sugar, continuing to whisk vigorously. Increase the speed to high and whip the meringue until glossy, soft peaks form.

6 Carefully spread the brown sugar meringue over the chocolate chips in the pan with a spatula (it will be very sticky, but do your best to spread it as evenly as possible).

7 Transfer the pan to the oven and bake until the top is golden and the edges pull away from the sides of the pan, 25 to 30 minutes. If the meringue layer looks like it's scorching, cover it with a piece of foil greased with butter or cooking spray.

8 Allow the cookie to cool completely before using the parchment overhang to lift it out of the pan and cutting it into small squares.

9 Serve at room temperature.

BROWNIE CANDY CUPS

I DEBATED CALLING THIS SECTION OF THE BOOK "ways to stuff chocolate into more chocolate," but, I don't know, it doesn't quite roll off the tongue the way I'd like it to. Here, we'll bake individual (hooray! No sharing necessary) brownie cups and stuff them with miniature candy bars, because chocolate on chocolate is always a good idea. This is a fun use of any leftover ("leftover!" ha) Halloween or Easter candy, and a great recipe to make with kids. Or, you know, adults. I'm not judging you.

9 ounces bittersweet chocolate, finely chopped, or 1½ cups bittersweet or dark chocolate chips

2 sticks (8 ounces) unsalted butter, melted (and still hot)

1½ cups powdered sugar

4 large eggs

1 tablespoon pure vanilla extract

1 teaspoon kosher salt

1 cup all-purpose flour

8 ounces miniature candy bars, roughly chopped (I like a mix of Kit Kats, Reese's, Snickers, and Twix bars)

1 Preheat the oven to 325°F, with a rack in the center position. Mist a 12-cup muffin tin with cooking spray.

2 Put the chocolate in a large heatproof bowl. Pour the hot melted butter over the chocolate and allow to sit until the chocolate is melted (about 1 minute), then stir together until smooth.

3 Sift the powdered sugar into the mixture and whisk to combine. Whisk in the eggs one at a time, then the vanilla. Gently whisk in the salt and flour until just incorporated.

4 Distribute the batter among the muffin cups, filling each three-fourths full (you'll have some batter left over) and top the cups with chopped candy. Transfer to the oven and bake until the brownie tops look dry and crackly, and a tester inserted into the center comes out with just a few moist crumbs, 12 to 15 minutes.

5 Allow the brownies to cool for about 25 minutes before turning them out of the pan and serving, either slightly warm or at room temperature.

6 The brownies will keep, tightly wrapped in plastic or foil, at room temperature for 4 to 5 days. They'll last a few months if frozen.

ACKNOWLEDGMENTS

Despite my occasional pleading,
it turns out that cookbooks don't just write
themselves, and I've got a lot of people
to thank for helping me pull this one off.
Thank you a million times over:

TO YOU! For picking up this book, and maybe even cooking from it. Thanks for trusting me with dinner (and perhaps dessert, too).

TO THE READERS OF DUNK & CRUMBLE, for the years of support and camaraderie. You're a pretty wonderful (and attractive) bunch.

TO ALYSSA REUBEN SEDRISH, for going to bat for me. Thanks for being the world's best agent.

TO AMANDA ENGLANDER (and the whole team at Clarkson Potter), for your faith in me, your tireless work, and your hilarious e-mails.

TO MATTHEW LASOF AND ALISON ADAIR, for all your hard work in the kitchen.

TO ARAN GOYOAGA AND JENN ELLIOTT BLAKE, for bringing this book to life.

TO MAGGIE GILBERT, recipe tester and consultant extraordinaire. I couldn't have done it without you.

TO MOM AND DAD, EM AND CASE, AND THE REST OF MY WONDERFUL FAMILY, thanks for being there always.

TO BEN AND CALDER, for your endless love and encouragement. Thanks for being my best guys.

INDEX